Advance Prai.. ior

Positive Parenting

"In this valuable contribution to parenting, Rebecca Eanes provides insightful, effective, and practical solutions to end family conflict and build loving connections. Her masterful approach allows parents to implement powerful strategies with ease and grace, forever transforming their family life. This is a must-read for every family that yearns to create peace and harmony." —Dr. Shefali Tsabary,
New York Times bestselling author of *The Conscious Parent*

"With a belief that each parent knows their own child best and that raising children should be enjoyable, not stressful, Rebecca Eanes helps parents develop their own positive parenting blueprints to create happy, loving families. *Positive Parenting* helps parents work through the difficult feelings that naturally occur throughout the parenting journey and provides strategies to help raise positive thinkers."
—Katie Hurley, LCSW,
author of *The Happy Kid Handbook*

"*Positive Parenting* is more than a parenting book. It's a guide to human connection. Rebecca provides a road map for creating happy, deeply connected families where children and parents alike are able to rise to their fullest potential." —Amy McCready,
author of *The "Me, Me, Me" Epidemic*

"As I soaked up the wisdom contained in this book, two words kept coming to mind: positive pathways. No matter how challenging your family situation is or how long you've been going down a negative road, this book offers pathways to peace, connection, and true happiness. Through practical examples, detailed steps, and soul-stirring

questions, Rebecca Eanes shows us how to reach our fullest potential as parents, partners, and human beings. Let *Positive Parenting* set you on a path to rewriting your story in all aspects of life, in the most positive way possible." —Rachel Macy Stafford,
New York Times bestselling author of
Hands Free Mama and *Hands Free Life*

"Rebecca Eanes has a deep understanding of what can hold mothers and fathers back from being the parents they want to be. *Positive Parenting* provides concrete tools to grow the self-discipline, connection, empathy, and techniques that will help parents (and their kids!) be their best." —Andrea Nair, MA, CCC,
psychotherapist, parenting educator,
and creator of the Taming Tantrums app

"Watch out: Eanes's book will transform your parenting, especially if you pause to do the self-work exercises." —Tracy Cutchlow,
author of *Zero to Five*

"In our always connected world of social media and Google searches there is a never-ending flow of 'new and better' parenting information. It's easy to get lost in the sea of 'best practices.' The focus is often on changing kids' behavior or all the reasons you are ruining your kids. The problem is that so much of what we read seems to conflict and leaves us feeling powerless rather than truly supporting parents and families. Rebecca's new book *Positive Parenting* emphasizes that parenting is far more than simply making kids comply. It's about real lives, relationships, and people; it's about real moms', dads', and kids' stories and how to make those stories incredible. This book gives the reader timeless, foundational principles and practices that help to build the parent, the child, and the family as a whole from the inside out." —Andy Smithson, www.truparenting.net

"*Positive Parenting* beautifully illustrates the choices that modern-day parents have to raise healthy and successful children through nurturing, empathetic relationships. Bolstered by research in neuroscience and human development, Eanes shows how parents must grow alongside their children, and how this parallel journey helps young people reach their full potential. This is a must-read book for all who care enough about their children to reflect deeply on themselves as parents."   —Marilyn Price-Mitchell, PhD,

author of *Tomorrow's Change Makers*

"In this one-of-a-kind book, Rebecca Eanes goes beyond just discipline to look at the big picture of parenting. If you're longing for more in your parenting journey—more joy, more peace, more cooperation—I recommend *Positive Parenting*!"   —Jessica Alexander,

coauthor of *The Danish Way of Parenting*

POSITIVE PARENTING

An Essential Guide

REBECCA EANES

Foreword by Dr. Laura Markham

A TarcherPerigee Book

An imprint of Penguin Random House LLC
375 Hudson Street, New York, New York 10014

Most TarcherPerigee books are available at special quantity discounts for bulk purchases for sales promotions, premiums, fund-raising, and educational use. Special books or book excerpts can also be created to fit specific needs. For details, write: SpecialMarkets@penguinrandomhouse.com.

Library of Congress Cataloging-in-Publication Data
Names: Eanes, Rebecca, author.
Title: Positive parenting : an essential guide / Rebecca Eanes.
Description: New York: TarcherPerigee, 2016.
Identifiers: LCCN 2016009096 (print) | LCCN 2016015873 (ebook) | ISBN 9780143109228 (paperback) | ISBN 9781101992203 (eBook)
Subjects: LCSH: Parenting. | Parent and child . | BISAC: FAMILY & RELATIONSHIPS / Parenting / Motherhood. | FAMILY & RELATIONSHIPS / Life Stages / Infants & Toddlers. | FAMILY & RELATIONSHIPS / Parenting / General.
Classification: LCC HQ755.8 .E176 2016 (print) | LCC HQ755.8 (ebook) | DDC 649/.1—dc23

First edition: June 2016

PRINTED IN THE UNITED STATES OF AMERICA

9   10

Text Design by Katy Riegel

This book is dedicated to my sons, who led me to a gentler path.

Thank you for loving me unconditionally while I figure out

how to be your mother. You are amazing people, and I

am honored to share in life's journey with you.

And to Eric, I'm forever grateful that we

are family. You are my happy place.

I love you all to the moon

and back.

Contents

Foreword

RAISING KIDS TO become emotionally healthy, happy, responsible adults is a formidable task. Parents tend to focus on those moments of crisis, when they wonder exactly what to say or how to teach a lesson. But they don't realize that they can prevent many of those crises by strengthening their relationship with their child. When children feel connected, nurtured, and confident that their parent is in charge and can meet their needs, they calm down and handle challenges and disappointments more easily. The number of crises diminishes and life gets smoother. And, amazingly, the parent discovers that she now knows intuitively just what to say or do when a crisis with her child does arise.

Of course, creating that strong, reassuring relationship with a child requires that the parent manage his own emotions. Nothing erodes the parent-child bond like a parent who throws his own tantrums or makes a child feel responsible for his big emotions. For parents who are seeking a more positive parenting style, this is often where they find themselves struggling. In fact, my experience with parents has shown me that this is by far the hardest part of raising children, which is already the toughest job most of us will ever do—one for which we receive zero training and very little support.

Positive Parenting, by Rebecca Eanes, is designed to give you that support, parent-to-parent. Rebecca understands that if we want our children to change, we must first change ourselves. Since children learn emotional regulation from our modeling, we must exercise our own self-discipline if we expect our children to do so. In the chapter "Important Self-Work," Rebecca takes parents on a journey of self-discovery that enables them to grow into their own fullest potential. She speaks from experience as a mother who took this challenge head-on, offering several strategies to help parents heal, grow, and gain the self-control needed to be positive parents.

One of the most frequent questions I hear from parents is "How do I get my partner on board?" Clearly, if one parent has committed to positive parenting while the other has not, conflicts will arise, which will disrupt the peace of the home and stress the parenting partnership. Eanes suggests parent-tested exercises for couples to build communication and cooperation, as well as thoughtful discussion questions at the end of every chapter that are designed to help couples work through conflicting perspectives and get on the same page.

Once you have united in your vision for your family, Eanes encourages you to create a blueprint so that you know exactly what kind of family you want to build and how to build it. Along the way, you'll learn communication skills that will strengthen your relationship with both your partner and your children. Eanes knows that peace on earth starts at home, and she gently guides you toward your goal of a peaceful home and a happy family with every page of this book.

Conventional parenting advice, which focuses on using discipline—punishment—to teach "lessons" to children, disconnects us as parents from our children, pitting us against them and creating a cycle of misbehavior and power struggles. Thankfully, there is a way to help children *want* to cooperate, which both strengthens your relationship with your child and guides him along the path of healthy development, throughout childhood and beyond.

So many parents I speak with are heartbroken and confused. They want to raise great children, but they hate how punishing their kids makes them feel. They don't want the disconnection or the heartache, but they're afraid of being too permissive. *Positive Parenting* shows parents how to remain connected while still being the leader every child needs. In the final chapters of this book, Rebecca discusses what she's learned about handling common behavior challenges with positive parenting. By changing the way we see behavior, we change how we respond to it—and our children change.

Connection truly is the key to putting the joy back into parenting. We intuitively long for it. Our hearts whisper it to us with every punishment, every power struggle, every raised voice, and yet we tune out the whispers of our hearts when we follow the cultural paradigm of shame, blame, and punishment. Rebecca offers the valuable insight of a mother who has made the shift to positive parenting. Her hard-earned wisdom comes straight from the trenches. She speaks to us parent-to-parent, gently encouraging us to listen to the whispers of our hearts, and giving us the tools for change.

Say good-bye to regrets and heartache and hello to peace and connection. Your beautiful journey begins here.

—Laura Markham, PhD,
author of *Peaceful Parent, Happy Kids*
and creator of AhaParenting.com

Introduction

PARENTHOOD. NOTHING BRINGS more elated joy or paralyzing fear. Nothing is as wonderful and daunting, soul lifting and heartbreaking, exhilarating and taxing as raising a child. And certainly nothing will stretch us, inspire us, and motivate us to better ourselves quite like being the person that little person looks up to.

Parenthood is sneaky. You think you're just raising a child, teaching this little person how to live and be in this lovely, chaotic world, but in truth, you're learning and growing right alongside him. If your heart remains open and your mind aware, you'll find that parenthood is the ultimate journey of self-discovery and that through raising this precious being who has been entrusted to your care, you rise to your own fullest potential.

I was six months pregnant with my first baby, and those first little flutters of movement had become real kicks! "You have to feel this!" I'd exclaim to my husband, who'd quickly scamper over and put his hand just where I laid it. We'd look into each other's eyes with excitement and wonder, and we'd wait. And wait. Nothing. He'd eventually move his hand away and, often only moments later, my son would kick again. When finally he did feel that little foot (or elbow) jabbing out of my skin, he responded with wide eyes and a quiet, "Wow, that's weird."

It *was* weird lying there watching my own tummy move and change shape. It was almost like a science fiction movie, and I could imagine an alien bursting out at any moment and slithering up the walls. I, of course, had seen the ultrasound pictures, the shape of a baby waving arms around and turning this way and that, and I felt the movements and the hiccups of a baby, but, at least for me, the fact that there was an actual chubby-cheeked, pink-lipped boy in there was just beyond my grasp.

All throughout my pregnancy, I would read to my little one. One book always brought me to tears. Perhaps it was the hormones, or perhaps it was the beginning of a deep realization of what was to come. I would grab *Guess How Much I Love You* from the bookshelf, fluff my pillows, sit back on my bed, rub my tummy, and read: *Little Nutbrown Hare, who was going to bed, held on tight to Big Nutbrown Hare's very long ears. He wanted to be sure that Big Nutbrown Hare was listening. "Guess how much I love you," he said. "Oh, I don't think I could guess that."*

Indeed, I couldn't guess at that moment just how much I loved this little boy poking around in my womb. I loved him already, to be sure, but just how much had not yet been revealed.

My little one came on his due date. I awoke at two a.m. with contractions that were strong and regular. Nine and a half hours later, he came out of my womb and into my arms. When my eyes first met his—what an incredible moment! There are no words to describe the awe and the love that flooded every cell of my being. It was simply miraculous.

If you are parents-to-be, you're in for quite a treat. Once you lay eyes on your little bundle, you will never be the same again. If you're already in the midst of babyhood, or toddlerhood, or childhood, you know the breadth of your love, and of your concerns, because once the smell of baby lotion, the nuzzling of a furry head in your neck, and the first coos and steps become a fond memory, you are hit with the realization that you are truly responsible for guiding this little human to adulthood. The question becomes—how on earth do I do this?

You have already shown your beautiful commitment to this responsibility by choosing this book. Your dedication and desire to build a connected family means you are already on the right track, and I commend your insight and effort to make your family the best it can be.

I'm so excited to share with you the wonderful news of positive parenting. I have great faith that every family who implements what I cover in this book will see improvement, not just in their child's behavior, but in their own behavior as well. You'll enjoy better family relationships and a significant increase in the joy of parenting. Positive parenting does raise healthy, well-adjusted, compassionate people, and the best part is you don't have to sacrifice family bonds to do it, as conventional parenting practices often do. In fact, positive parenting will strengthen not only your bond with your child, but your bond as a family unit, and that bond will last a lifetime.

The first step in effective parenting is to come together as a couple and commit to this road ahead. This book will lay down the path for each of you as it leads you on individual journeys of self-discovery before bringing you together to build your desired family. You'll discover many things about yourselves and about each other along the way. This requires commitment to each other, to your child, and to the ideals you set forth in your family blueprint in chapter 6. It's going to take some self-work and a good deal of working together, but the reward is priceless.

In this book, I suggest several therapeutic exercises for the purpose of self-growth. These are exercises I have done myself and found to be helpful in my journey. They may bring up difficult emotions in certain people. If you find that you have strong emotions or difficulty with these exercises, I suggest you seek the advice of a professional.

Positive parenting is a broad subject, and as with most other topics, opinions vary among proponents. **I am not a medical or psychological professional.** What I'm describing here is my unique perception of positive parenting, which is a culmination of countless hours of research, reading, studying, and soul-searching plus six years and counting of analysis and observation with my own cherished children, along with insights from fellow parents at my active and supportive community on Facebook, Positive Parenting: Toddlers and Beyond, which is currently more than 520,000 parents strong and growing fast.

I am not a medical or psychological professional.

I wish you and your sweet family all the best on this beautiful journey of parenthood.

The Goal of This Book

This is not yet another book telling you how you should or shouldn't discipline your children. **You are the experts on your own children**; I'm not. It will be up to you to decide what is right in any given situation. I will offer advice consistent with what has worked in my own family and with

You are the experts on your own children

what neuroscientists and psychologists have determined is effective in raising emotionally healthy, responsible kids, but please understand that this is parent-to-parent advice, not a rule book.

The ultimate goal is a healthy, connected family unit that benefits not just the children, but you, the parents, as well. The process starts with you, which is why we begin with doing the work to make yourself better. You are the person those little eyes are looking up to and learning from every day. As you learn to deactivate your triggers, gain confidence and self-discipline, and take charge of your life story, your entire family will reap the rewards.

The focus then turns to coming together as a couple, finding the middle ground that you both are comfortable with, learning to honor each other and communicate effectively, and improving your relationship, which is the cornerstone of your family.

Next, we discuss how to build a strong foundation for your connected family, and how to define your family unit through routines, traditions, and family culture. By being intentional, focused, and self-disciplined, you can make your dream of a happy, close family come to fruition.

Finally, the last chapters redefine discipline as you learn to move past knee-jerk reactions and ineffective punishment to solution-oriented discipline that truly teaches and inspires your child to become the best version of himself or herself. I discuss the top five behaviors that trigger parents and offer suggestions for dealing with those behaviors the positive-parenting way.

At the end of each chapter you will find a list of discussion questions. These are meant to be worked through together with your partner for the purpose of developing better communication skills, finding common ground, and deepening your bond as a couple. These questions are important, and while it may be tempting to skip over them to continue reading, I hope you'll take the time to work through them together.

Following the questions, you'll find a section called "Putting It into Practice." This will teach you how to put the ideas set forth in the chapter into action in your home. Some sections offer extra tips and exercises for you to try with your loved ones.

My hope is that by the end of this book, you will have a better understanding of yourselves, each other, and your relationship, and a focus for building your connected family.

I invite you to join our growing Facebook community, Positive Parenting: Toddlers and Beyond, if you haven't already done so. There, you'll find support, encouragement, and information to assist you in meeting your parenting goals.

POSITIVE PARENTING

1

The Positive
Parenting Philosophy

Many people think that discipline is the essence of
parenting. But that isn't parenting. Parenting is not
telling your child what to do when he or she
misbehaves. Parenting is providing the conditions
in which a child can realize his or her full human
potential.   —Gordon Neufeld

I HAD FALLEN into a trap. Caught in the net of societal expectations, I surrendered my inner voice. Rather than doing what I
felt in my heart was right, I did what magazines, family members, and experts told me was right. Yet, it always felt so wrong.

Here's the problem. I believe we are meant to enjoy our children and the days we are blessed to spend with them. Children
are gifts, but rather than joyfully unwrapping the miracle of
this life we have been chosen to be a part of, so many of us fall
into the pit of just trying to manage our kids' behavior. The
fleeting days of a quiet and immobile infant give way to a little
person full of energy and attitude, and with toddlerhood comes
all sorts of warnings about the days ahead—terrible twos, threen-
agers, fearsome fours, and so on. With these dire warnings
come loads of advice from every angle telling us how to keep

our children in line. So, the whispers of our hearts get drowned out by the noisiness of everyone telling us how we should raise our children.

We've bought into this extremely negative perception of children and their motives. We dote on and swoon over babies, but before even twenty-four months have passed, we are led to believe that these sweet, innocent babes will become tyrants who will try to overthrow our authority and take over our homes! Consider the negative messages that are so prevalent in our society:

- We are led to believe that a child—even an infant—who cannot sleep on her own is trying to manipulate us for attention. We are advised to end this swiftly by ignoring a crying child so that she can learn to self-soothe and to immediately and consistently return her to her bed if she seeks comfort in ours. Yet, this tiny human, only months to a few short years old, is simply seeking what she knows instinctually she must have—closeness with her parents.
- Tantrums are viewed as a child's calculated and devious attempt at getting our attention or their own way, and again we are told to ignore the child so that we do not reinforce this negative behavior. Only a couple of years out of the womb and we see him as a duplicitous mastermind rather than a young human lacking coping and communication skills who needs the help and guidance of his caregiver.
- During the toddler years, what is actually normal development is seen as a testing of our authority. We are told that we absolutely must put our iron fists down hard and heavy or else they'll run right over us.

These are the "truths" society has accepted about children. So, as soon as possible, we are told, we must exert our control and show them who's boss. Overpowering our children works fairly well for a short while. We certainly have the advantage of size, strength, and a fully developed brain. Sooner or later, though, the child starts to push back. Then begins the never-ending struggle for power that is modern-day parenting.

These daily power struggles usually not only put a strain on the parent-child relationship, but as tensions rise and parents become worn out and frustrated, marriages can suffer. Arguments erupt over how to effectively discipline the child, and differences in theory and practice often drive a wedge between parents. Our hunger for the control we are told we must always maintain chomps away, bit by bit, at our attachments with our children and even with our partners.

Why do we feel so angry and out of control? Because we can only hold on to the control for so long, and when we feel it slipping away, we panic, resorting to yelling, threatening, and punishing. The cycle continues to spiral down and down until all the joy has been zapped from the relationships we have with those precious little ones we held in our arms not so long ago.

The more I wielded my parental power, the worse he behaved, and the more disconnected we became.

I know, because I was that parent. There was a time when my days had become so focused on disciplining every wrongdoing that there was no joy left in our day. My son and I were miserable. **The more I wielded my parental power, the worse he behaved, and the more disconnected we became.** I had become ensnared in the joyless parenting trap that so many others are caught in. Now that I am free, I want to cut the ropes and free everyone else.

In 2010, I started an online community via Facebook called Positive Parenting: Toddlers and Beyond. The community was born out of my desire to connect with other parents who, like me, wanted to choose a different path but weren't quite sure which way to turn. What a tremendous blessing it has been to see the community grow to now more than 520,000 members. Hundreds of thousands of parents have discovered the power of positive parenting, and this movement isn't slowing down. We gain about eight thousand new parents every single week! Positive parenting gave me back the connection with my son that I had lost. It brought so much peace and joy to our home, and it has done the same for countless other families.

Katrina shared a similar story on my Facebook page. "Positive parenting saved my relationship with my son and my sanity," she said. "After holding his thrashing little body in time-out for the tenth time in a day, I wondered what was wrong with my child or why I was a failure as a parent because I couldn't control my child perfectly. Positive parenting gave me the new perspective and the strategies I needed to bring back our happy home."

I suspect many more parents are feeling the same as Katrina and I felt—missing the joy they had in those first several months as they bonded with their new baby. I was so relieved when I discovered positive parenting. As I read about the philosophy, a heavy weight was lifted from me, and as I implemented this in my own family, I saw an unbelievable transformation. That's why I'm writing this book. I want to share this information with you so that you, too, can let go of fear and control and tap into the wellspring of love and connection.

I love the story that Robin shared with me. Robin knew that she didn't want to use traditional parenting methods, but she was at a loss as to how to discipline her child any other way. She told me that once she started using positive parenting practices, her entire household felt so much more peaceful and pleasant and she began enjoying her time with her daughter a lot more. She has a better relationship with her child now, and her child is very well behaved. What tugged at my heart the most was when Robin shared this with me: "Handling my child with love and respect made me take a closer look at myself and how I handle my own emotions. Using positive parenting has literally made me a better parent—calmer, more patient, and more empathetic." What a wonderful testimony to the power of positive parenting to change lives!

What Is Positive Parenting?

Positive parenting is a philosophy rooted in connection. It isn't just a method of discipline, but an entirely different way of relating to children that allows us to maintain a strong bond with them through the ages and stages of childhood while still raising kind and responsible people.

Conventional parenting methods often pit parent against child, as though we are adversaries in a never-ending struggle for power and position. This naturally leads to disconnection between family members

Conventional parenting methods often pit parent against child

and discontent in the home. Thankfully, it doesn't have to be that way! By using positive parenting in your home, you can maintain the deep connection you are meant to have as you work with, not against, your child to guide him or her along the journey to adulthood. With strong connection comes more co-operation, and with that, more joy and peace in the family.

Many people question whether this is permissive parenting, and the answer is absolutely not. Permissive parents do not set and enforce limits; positive parents do. While I understand how challenging it can be at first to learn how to enforce limits without resorting to punishment, rest assured that **an absence of punishment is not the same as an absence of discipline**. In fact, the very reason I do not punish my children is because life's messes cannot be fixed with a nose in the corner. They will take responsibility for their actions by making amends, righting wrongs, solving the problems they create, and learning how to make better choices in the future. A child does not learn self-discipline by sitting, but by doing. Once the paradigm shift is made and you understand that all discipline is simply teaching, it becomes easy to guide a child without punishment.

An absence of punishment is not the same as an absence of discipline

The Five Principles of Positive Parenting

The foundation of positive parenting rests on five principles: attachment, respect, proactive parenting, empathetic leadership, and positive discipline. These five principles go hand in hand to both build a strong bond and to position you to be the effective leader your child needs to guide him through childhood.

1. Attachment

According to the attachment bond theory pioneered by English psychiatrist John Bowlby and American psychologist Mary Ainsworth, the bond (or attachment) formed between primary caregivers and infants is responsible for:

- shaping all our future relationships
- strengthening or damaging our ability to focus, be conscious of our feelings, and calm ourselves
- affecting our ability to bounce back from misfortune.[1]

Children are hardwired to connect on a biochemical level. This happens first with their immediate family and then with the broader community. If that connection isn't there, the brain may not develop as it is supposed to. When a secure attachment is made, the child feels safe. Research suggests that children who fail to develop a secure attachment in the early years often have behavioral problems and relationship troubles later in life.[2]

2. Respect

As human beings, children deserve the same consideration we afford to others. Children need to be treated in a thoughtful, civil, and courteous manner, just as we treat other people. Research[3] has shown that children who have loving, nurturing parents grow a bigger hippocampus, which promotes better memory, learning, and stress response. Therefore, we respect a child's mind when we are nurturing and positive. We respect a child's body and dignity when we choose not to hit her to cause deliberate pain for training purposes. We respect her person-hood when we give space to allow her to explore and develop at her own pace. We respect her spirit, acknowledging that each child comes with her own unique spirit, which is to be honored.

3. Proactive parenting

Proactive parents address potential problem behavior at the first sign, before it becomes a serious problem. We also understand that by putting in extra time building the relationship and teaching up front, we thwart many problems that could have arisen from disconnection and lack of knowledge and instruction. Proactive parenting also means that parents respond rather than react to their children's behaviors. This requires forethought into how one will respond as well as a planned action. Whereas reactive parents act impulsively, responsive parents are in control of themselves and able to execute the plan when a situation arises.

4. Empathetic leadership

Not to be confused with permissive parents, positive parents are still in the leadership role. In fact, it is a gross disservice to children to not give them competent leaders to guide them on their journeys in this big, new world. Being empathetic means we understand the needs of our children and relate to them in a way that helps them feel heard and understood while still holding the boundaries we have set.

5. Positive discipline

Punishment is distinct from discipline. The goal of punishment is to make someone suffer enough to cause them to want to avoid that particular behavior (and therefore punishment) again in the future. The goal of discipline is to teach someone to control impulses and behavior, to learn new skills, and to fix mistakes and find solutions.

Many of today's "parenting methods" focus entirely on how to discipline children. The philosophy of positive parenting goes way beyond just discipline. While the actions and demeanor you take in discipline are important, realize it is not just discipline that matters but the entire childhood experience you provide. Children are shaped not only in moments of admonition and correction but by the hundreds of thousands of moments—smiles and tears, successes and failures, encouragement and discouragement, laughter and sorrow, acceptance and denial, disconnects and reconnects—that make up their childhood.

Brain Science 101

I refer to the upstairs (thinking) brain and the downstairs (reptilian) brain several times in this book. These are terms used by Drs. Daniel Siegel and Tina Payne Bryson as a simplified way to describe the parts and functions of the brain. I'd like to briefly explain what these terms mean.

I believe that understanding the basic functions of the brain and how the brain develops in children is an important part of the paradigm shift for many parents. It certainly was for me.

Without this knowledge, it is difficult to see why we believe what we believe about behavior.

As I stated, I am not a professional, so I look to Dr. Daniel Siegel, neuropsychiatrist, and parenting expert Tina Payne Bryson, PhD, who are the pioneering experts behind *The Whole-Brain Child* and *No-Drama Discipline*.

This is an extremely simplistic model of a very complex organ, but basically, according to Siegel and Bryson, the downstairs brain is made up of the brain stem and the limbic region, which together form the lower sections of the brain. The brain stem is well developed at birth. It is the primitive part of our brain, responsible for our most fundamental mental and neural operations: strong emotions, instincts, and basic functions such as breathing and digestion.

The upstairs brain is responsible for more sophisticated and complex thinking, but is underdeveloped at birth and begins to grow during infancy and childhood. Unlike the primitive, downstairs brain, the upstairs brain is responsible for thinking, emotional, and relational skills that allow us to live balanced, meaningful lives and enjoy healthy relationships.[4]

This information is key to understanding behaviors such as tantrums and aggression because when you realize that a toddler simply does not have the cognitive capability to pause and reflect (a function of the underdeveloped upstairs brain), suddenly you understand that this isn't poor behavior but purely an issue of brain development. This knowledge helps us provide empathy and understanding in situations that would otherwise cause us a lot of frustration.

This is not to say we ignore the behavior, writing it off as a problem that will self-correct with brain development, but rather we use this knowledge to gain a better understanding of our children so that we can guide their behavior more effectively.

Supportive Research

Whole books have been written on this, and a plethora of articles can be found from neuroscientists and psychologists who have spent their careers studying the effects of attachment, the parent-child bond, punishment and shame and their effects on the human psyche, and so forth. I recommend reading Siegel and Bryson's *The Whole-Brain Child*, and *The Science of Parenting*, by Margot Sunderland, as well as looking up the works of Alfie Kohn, Allan Schore, and Gordon Neufeld for a more in-depth look at the science behind this philosophy. I will, however, provide a concise overview.

We now know the incredible role that attachment plays in the healthy development of our children. We know that our earliest relationships actually build the brain structures we use for relating to others our whole lives. We know that the experiences in those early relationships encode in the neural circuitry of our brains by twelve to eighteen months of age, entirely in the implicit memory, and that these patterns of attachment become the "rules" for relating to other humans that we will go on to use for the rest of our lives. We know that when those early experiences have been less than optimal, those unconscious patterns of attachment can continue to shape our responses and perceptions throughout the rest of our lives unless we consciously create new patterns.[5]

Simply put, we, the parents, set the precedent for how human relationships are for our children. We can set the standard high or low, to be respectful or disrespectful, to be encouraging or discouraging. This is why it is so important that we strive for healthy, respectful, and compassionate relationships with our children now, so that they will not seek out or accept unhealthy relationships later.

Connection is vital because the human brain is literally wired to connect, and when that connection isn't happening, we suffer emotionally. Furthermore, when we experience social pain—isolation, disapproval, or a cruel word—the feeling is as real as physical pain.

Scientist Matthew Lieberman says, "Across many studies of mammals, from the smallest rodents all the way to us humans, the data suggests that we are profoundly shaped by our social environment and that we suffer greatly when our social bonds are threatened or severed. When this happens in childhood it can lead to long-term health and educational problems. We may not like the fact that we are wired such that our well-being depends on our connections with others, but the facts are the facts."[6]

None of us set out to cause our children emotional, physical, or educational harm. Our parents didn't know that spanking us could affect the gray matter in our brains,[7] which influences intelligence, learning abilities, sensory perception, speech, muscular control, emotions, and memory. They had no idea that fear releases hormones that can be toxic to the brain. Most of this research on attachment has occurred in the past twenty years, so the generations before us simply didn't have access to this information. Now that we do know, we have the responsibility to make the necessary changes in the way we raise our children to ensure that we send forth the healthiest human beings possible.

It's easy to ignore the scientific research in favor of what we've always been told. It's simple to just continue doing what we have always done—what our families and friends have always done. Doing so is an injustice to our children and to future generations. They deserve the best we have to give them using the knowledge available to us, even if it means we have to learn new ways to be.

Ignoring all of the attachment and brain development research is like ignoring the research on smoking. Just as some people will continue to smoke despite the known risks, some parents will continue to use harsh discipline. Just as some smokers will not get lung cancer, some children raised with harsh discipline will not have lasting psychological damage. The question is, are you a gambler? And how much are you willing to risk?

Discussion Questions

1. What was your perception of positive parenting before reading this chapter?
2. Do you think society views children in a negative manner? What messages have you been fed about young children and what they need in terms of discipline?
3. Can you think of a few times when you reacted with your "downstairs brain"—in a moment of anger or another emotion—only to later revisit the situation with your "upstairs brain" to solve the problem in a more rational and productive way?

Putting It into Practice

Positive parenting begins with practicing the five principles outlined in the chapter: attachment, respect, proactive parenting, empathetic leadership, and positive discipline. Let's break down what this looks like in daily life.

Attachment

No matter your child's age, attachment is formed by being *lovingly responsive* to the child's needs. Secure attachment refers to the child's emotional experience, not your own sense of connection. This is why it is important to be able to read your child's cues to determine her needs, whether she is three months, three years, or thirteen years old. Tips for developing secure attachment:

- Respond promptly and lovingly to cries or emotional upsets.
- Understand your child's cues for food, rest, play, and comfort, and attend to them accordingly.
- Give full, focused attention without distractions. Be present in the moment.
- Provide lots of positive attention—talking, laughing, play, cuddles.

We typically think of attachment as it relates to infants, but young children do not outgrow the need for secure attachment by toddlerhood. While you instinctively respond to your baby's cries, you may feel like you should ignore the cries of a two-year-old or tell a ten-year-old to stop crying because whatever he's upset about isn't a big deal. Yet, responding lovingly even to the two- and ten-year-old is what keeps the attachment bond strong. That bond is jeopardized when we ignore or mock a child's cries. I discuss how to lovingly respond to tantrums without giving in to demands in chapter 10. In regard to understanding cues, this is a staple of positive parenting throughout all stages. Learning our baby's cues for sleep, food, play, comfort, and so on is a stepping-stone to understanding the more complex needs of a toddler, preschooler, and beyond. In fact, understanding cues helps tremendously with discipline as we assess the need behind the behavior in question. This includes reading cues from your teen concerning the need for privacy, quality time, and more. **Loving responsiveness isn't just for babies.** It's the cornerstone of a secure attachment throughout all of childhood.

> *Loving responsiveness isn't just for babies.*

Respect

There are many ways to demonstrate respect to your child. Remember, by experiencing respect, children learn to show respect to others.

- Practice good communication skills—be a good listener. More on this in chapter 4.
- Respect their bodies. It's probably tempting to lick your finger and wipe a smudge off his face, but would you be grossed out if someone did that to you? I would. We also

unconsciously do things like swoop toddlers up without warning, brush or fix their hair without asking, etc. A good rule of thumb is to ask yourself if you'd like having it done to you without permission or warning.

- Allow them to make choices. Children are basically bossed around all day, and then we wonder why we have power struggles. Allowing them to make decisions about little things throughout their day helps them feel like they have some control and shows that you respect them.
- Be honest. You don't have to spill every detail if it isn't age appropriate to do so, but you don't have to lie either. If you want open, honest communication from your child, model it.
- Apologize when you've wronged them. This goes a long way toward showing your child that you have respect for him—and it models good behavior for when he wrongs someone else.
- Respect their space and privacy according to your good judgment.
- Avoid embarrassing them in front of their peers, in public, or online.
- Speak kindly about them to others, especially in their presence.

Showing respect to children is no different from showing respect to anyone else. We do not put them down, shame them, speak in a rude or disrespectful manner, threaten violence, or hit them. Those are not "tough love" parenting techniques; they are bullying techniques. Children learn what they live, and if those techniques are used on them, they are likely to use them on someone else—imagining that they have your stamp of approval because you showed them how to do it.

Proactive Parenting

I think of proactive parenting in two ways: (1) catching a potential problem before it gets out of hand, and (2) having a plan of action for when a problem arises. For example, if three-year-old Jenny is beginning to show signs of aggression during playdates, the proactive parent would start (or kick up a notch) teaching Jenny about emotion management, create a "calm-down area" for her, and set a limit of no aggressive behavior. The parent might print out some feelings faces to talk about with Jenny, act out a skit in a sock puppet show, and have her help to create a calm-down jar. When Jenny shows the first sign of aggression the next time, the limit is upheld by taking her to "time-in," or her calm-down area. Time-in is discussed more in chapter 9. Mom or Dad knows in advance what steps to take when aggression happens so she or he is able to calmly handle the situation with ease.

To put this into practice, set important boundaries early, be aware of changes in your child's behaviors and of potential problem behaviors, and create your own plan of action for dealing with unwanted behaviors, particularly those that trigger your own anger.

Empathetic Leadership

Empathy is the key that unlocks your child's brain when he is upset and allows your reason to get inside. Enforcing limits and correcting behavior is a part of parenting, and positive parents know it's an important part of parenting. We also know that empathy calms the brain and reaches straight to a child's heart, which makes him open to receive our wisdom and instruction. Empathy shows your child that you understand his feelings, and that you are on his side. Note the difference in these two reactions to Cole throwing a ball inside and breaking a vase.

Reaction 1 (without empathy): Cole! You know throwing a ball inside is against the rules! I can't believe you were so careless! You're grounded for a week!

Reaction 2 (with empathy): Uh-oh! You broke the vase. You must be feeling pretty bad about it. I see tears in your eyes. This is why we had the rule about not throwing the ball in the house. It's unfortunate, but mistakes happen. How are you going to fix this?

Which reaction is going to shut Cole down? Which one is more likely to solve the problem?

Positive Discipline

It is often tempting to respond to misbehavior with anger, aggression, shaming, and conventional means of punishment (time-outs, spanking, and other techniques). But I believe there's a better approach—one that doesn't diminish your child, and one that makes the most of the teaching opportunity that misbehavior presents us. Here are my three steps to positive discipline.

Step One: Assess the need. All behavior is an indication of the internal state of the child. Misbehavior is a cue that there is an underlying need. When we assess what that need is and address it, often the misbehavior vanishes. This can be tricky with toddlers and preschoolers who cannot yet verbalize their needs or intentions, but just understanding that the behavior is a call for help rather than a calculated act of defiance of your authority can help you be compassionate and responsive. Sometimes the need is easy to determine, such as hunger or tiredness, which can be cured with a meal or a nap. Other times, the behavior is signaling the need for a new boundary or to learn a skill, or possibly that there is something going on outside the home that your child is having trouble dealing with. For example, a toddler who has discovered the joy of jumping on the couch isn't trying to misbehave. She's playing. Even so, you probably don't want her to jump on the couch, but when you tell her to stop, she doesn't. This is signaling the need for a new boundary. Another example is a school-aged child who is suddenly showing signs of aggression or displaying a disrespectful attitude after school. Yes, the behavior must be corrected, but this is a clear sign that something is amiss inside the child. Finding out what is motivating the aggression or disrespect and helping her resolve the problem will end the bad behavior.

Step Two: Calm yourself and your child. Undisciplined parents cannot effectively discipline children, so calm yourself down first (more on that in chapter 2). Move from emotionally reactive to cognitively responsive before you deal with the problem at hand. Once calm, help your child become calm. The goal is to engage his upstairs brain so that he is no longer emotionally reactive but able to reason. This could take two minutes or twenty minutes, depending on the child and her stage of development. Time-in is helpful to calm the brain because of the close contact with you and soothing exercises such as reading and drawing. Some children may resist a time-in and prefer to be left alone. If this works to calm them, that's good. We don't want to force separation, as that can erode our connection, but giving a child the space he's asking for is respecting his needs. You are ready to teach the lesson once your child is showing receptiveness toward you again.

Step Three: Teach and problem-solve. For children under four, problem solving is too much to expect of them. The cognitive development to work through this process hasn't happened yet, though certainly the parent can talk through it as he or she solves the problem, for modeling purposes. For young children, holding the limit by removing the child from the situation or removing the object that is being thrown, for example, is enough. Teaching what the child can do is also appropriate for very young children. "I won't let you throw in the house, but you can throw this ball in the yard." "I won't let you hit. You may stomp and wiggle the angries out." When your child is between roughly four and six, you can start teaching her how to problem-solve. Ask the following questions to get the ball rolling:

- What caused this to happen?
- How did this make you feel?
- What can you do the next time this happens?
- How are you going to fix this?

2

Important Self-Work

The stories we tell ourselves have great power over
us. Depending on how they are told, our stories can
either enlighten or mislead, inspire or discourage.
                                            —Mike Bellah

ON THE DAY you were born, a fresh new story began. A book
of blank pages waiting to be filled was given to your parents.
For the first several years of your life, the experiences they provided you were written down on those fresh pages. They—your
parents, or the other adults who raised you—are the authors of
your earliest chapters. As time passed, more "authors" started
penning their own parts to your story. Siblings, teachers,
friends, and companions have all added to your book. Everything you have experienced right up to this moment—and sig-
nificantly, how you have perceived everything that you have
experienced—is bound together, attached to your identity, and
coded in your brain circuitry. Our stories are powerful. They
define who we are and the way we conduct ourselves. They color
the lens through which we view the world.

Unconsciously, we can continue well into adulthood letting others fill the pages while we sit idly by, or we can take ownership of our stories and challenge what has been written by others without our permission. Just as you might take a red pen and correct errors in a manuscript to refine and improve the story, so you can bring your own story to light and make the necessary corrections in your mind where you see errors that are holding you back. You had absolutely no control over those pages filled in by your family in your earliest days, but what's great is that you do have the control now over your perceptions of those first chapters and the ones who wrote them.

Consider the story of Elijah. He was born to a distant and detached mother, who wrote on his first pages that he was unlovable and worthless. Elijah saw himself as his mother saw him, as children often do. He developed a very poor self-concept as a result of her detachment. Because of this, he often had trouble forming meaningful relationships. With a one-two punch of being distrustful and feeling unlovable, he pushed people away without recognizing the patterns he kept repeating. His failure at forming relationships with others further solidified his negative view of himself.

One day, at the age of nineteen, Elijah was lucky enough to encounter someone who could see his light—the good that was within him. This person saw his worth and challenged him to read over the first chapters of his story. In doing so, he realized that his mother was detached because of her own personal story and not because there was something wrong with him. He had been an innocent baby born into an unfortunate circumstance. He now felt compassion for the child he once was, and he knew that little boy deserved a better story. This shift allowed Elijah to see himself in a different light, the light that was reflected on him by someone who could see it in him all along. His feelings of self-worth grew, and he was able to take the pen and fill his present pages with happier stories, which bode well for a brighter future for Elijah.

Who do you want to be? When you imagine your best self, what does that look like? Like Elijah did, intentionally thinking about our own stories can help us understand why we think, react, and behave in the habitual ways that we do. Focused self-reflection about where we come from help us to understand ourselves, question our relationship patterns, and challenge our beliefs. This is the beginning of growth.

Consider the following questions: How was your childhood? What are the events and relationships that shaped who you are today? What have been the turning points in your life? Which relationships (other than the one with your parents) mattered most in the formation of how you relate to those closest to you now? What successes and failures have created your current outlook about the possibilities for your future? What beliefs do you have about children and child-rearing?

Take some time to truly reflect on those questions, and talk them through with your partner. Then, if you'd like, write out your life story on paper. Begin with your earliest memories and just let the story flow without being critical about what you are writing down. Include everything that you feel is relevant to who you are today and who you want to be, particularly concentrating on what influenced your current beliefs about relationships.

Once you have your story written down, take a red pen or highlighter and mark the parts of your story that you feel need

You are holding the pen now. You get to decide if you'll be a hero.

to be rewritten—the parts that you feel aren't serving you well in your quest to be the best partner and parent you can be. This is owning your story. You aren't denying your past or pretending that certain things happened when they never did (or vice versa). Rather, you are simply looking at it objectively from an adult point of view and declaring that your past will not rule your present. **You are holding the pen now. You get to decide if you'll be a hero.**

Rewriting my story has been one of the most powerful exercises I've done in my journey of self-growth. As is true with everyone, my personal story is full of ups and downs, wins and losses, accomplishments and struggles. There was one particular struggle that I had allowed to define me for years. It had seeped all the way down and rooted itself in my identity. I felt trapped in its grip, like there was no escape. I believed I would never overcome it or be the same again. *That struggle had become my story.* I was stuck on the same, never-ending chapter of despair, and I seriously wanted to turn the page.

I came across this idea of rewriting our stories and was intrigued, so I gave it a try. Although, as I said, we cannot undo our pasts or change what happened to us, we can choose to see through a new lens. We can look at our stories from different angles and with different perceptions and find the strength, courage, and resilience we had that got us through.

Now that you are aware of how your past has influenced you, you can choose to frame your experiences in a new way, just as I did, so that you can release your baggage and move forward.

Here are some tips for becoming the author of your own story.

1. Review your story. This is what we have been doing in this section. Don't sugarcoat it. Say, "This is what happened to me. It shaped me in this way. I have the power now to change." Finding even a smidgen of positivity in very bad experiences ("I survived," "It made me stronger," "I learned how not to be") can be very helpful.

2. Express gratitude. Whatever the circumstances were, you are here now. You have a desire to improve, and that is a great sign of strength. You are learning new skills, and you are capable of positive change.

3. Notice where you lay blame. "I have an explosive temper because of my mother." "I can't express emotions because of my father." "I don't trust men/women because of that certain boyfriend/girlfriend." When we can stop playing the blame game and take ownership of our behaviors, we free ourselves to move forward.

4. Ask yourself what will happen if you stay stuck where you are. Get a detailed image in your mind of how your life will be a decade from now if you continue living as you are. What will your relationship with your child look like? With your partner? Will you be burdened with regrets? Now imagine that you've become the person you want to be and have been living *that* life for a decade. What do your relationships look like? This was a very powerful exercise for me. If you really envision these two separate outcomes in vivid detail, this exercise can be a life changer.

5. Now that you have a clear vision of the future you want for yourself and your family, rewrite your story in a way that empowers you. Write yourself strong. Write yourself capable. Write yourself victorious. If you've written both stories on pa-

per, crumple up your old one and toss it in the trash, or burn it for a more powerful release. Letting your old story go is a brave and necessary step toward becoming the person, partner, and parent you want to become.

6. Make your new story a reality by changing your thought patterns. When you shift your thoughts, your feelings shift, and following in line are your actions. It sounds simple enough, but forging new neural pathways can be hard work. I have four steps to help you succeed, which you will find later in this chapter.

As for my own story, I was honest with myself about my struggle and the huge toll it had taken on me and my relationships, but I also began to be honest about what my life was before that struggle. I had become so wrapped up in it that I could no longer see who I had been. I realized that this wasn't who I was but rather something that I had gone through—an *experience*, not an *existence*. Not my identity, just something that happened to me.

Is that something that you can perhaps relate to? Has an experience become your existence?

As I rewrote my story, I decided that trial would not be the final chapter. I wrote myself overcoming the years-long struggle, even though I hadn't yet overcome it. I wrote the next chapter of my life, and the one I envisioned after that.

That simple exercise gave me a new perspective on my experience, and helped me to see there was a better future ahead. I just had to grasp it. Sometimes we can't stop rereading the chapter we're in, and that prevents us from moving on. That struggle is now a part of my story, but not my whole story. I went on to be the overcomer I wrote myself to be. I want you to know that I believe you can, too.

Note: If this exercise brings up strong emotions for you, you may want to do it under the care of a licensed therapist. If you experienced abuse or trauma in your childhood, seek professional counseling for help in healing.

Changing Your Thought Patterns

I used to have a lot of negative thoughts whirring around in my head every single day. It was a like a record that played over and over, and the record began playing as soon as I opened my eyes from what little sleep I'd managed to get the night before. *Oh, great. Morning already. I'm not ready to do this again today. I'm still exhausted from yesterday. When do I get a break?* These poisonous thoughts started my day off on a sour note, and it usually went downhill from there. I had negative thoughts about my ability to parent, negative thoughts about how little sleep I was getting, and negative thoughts about having negative thoughts!

Our thoughts have a very real impact on our demeanor and how we treat those around us. Every single time I allowed myself to think those toxic thoughts, they burrowed deeper and deeper into my brain, causing my default thinking to be poisonous to myself and my family. This is one of the most challenging endeavors I've taken on; however, if I want to give my best to my family, it's worth developing better thought patterns. My negative thoughts left me feeling fatigued, irritable, and disappointed. I wanted my children to have a joyful mother, yet how can one be joyful with a toxic inner monologue running all day long? No longer wanting to live in a state of perpetual negativity, I started to do some research.

Studies have shown that we can actively affect how our brains rewire themselves to create new neural networks and override preexisting ones. The way to build new neural networks is by going off the beaten path—changing our thought patterns.[8]

This is wonderful news for anyone who, like me, needs to kick some habitual negative thoughts. Do any of these sound familiar?

- I'm terrible at this.
- Nobody appreciates me.
- Being a parent is too hard.
- She's such a whiny kid. I'm so sick of hearing her whine over everything.
- He's never going to get potty trained. Why can he not get this?

Not only are these negative thoughts a downer to our days, but they actually mess with our brain chemicals, causing unwanted negative emotions. These emotions, in turn, affect our behavior if we aren't careful, and we end up poorly treating the targets of our negative thoughts—often our children, our partners, or ourselves.

Are you generally a positive thinker? If you are, that's wonderful! If not, that's okay, too. You can make yourself a positive thinker! Need motivation? What goes through your mind usually comes out of your mouth, and what comes out of your mouth usually goes into little ears. What goes into little ears often becomes what goes through little minds and out of little mouths.

If we want to raise positive thinkers, we have to learn to be positive thinkers. We have to be willing to own our stories, our thoughts, our feelings, and our behaviors. That's how we grow into our fullest potential as people and as parents. Having the strength of will to command your thoughts shows great maturity and is one of the keys to a happier life and a more connected family. The question is, how can we become positive thinkers?

If we want to raise positive thinkers, we have to learn to be positive thinkers.

Over the past few years, I've spent much time researching the effects of positive and negative thinking and how to change thought patterns long term, and the following is what I've learned:

Think of neural pathways as trenches that keep getting deeper each time a pattern of thought is given attention or interest. If you've spent many years giving attention to negative thought patterns (this could be anything from *I'm clumsy* to *My child is so difficult*), there will be a deep trench (neural pathway) in your brain for these thoughts. Since the brain has a tendency to repeat thought patterns that have strong neural pathways, it becomes a vicious cycle of reinforcement. You have a negative thought, the trench deepens, and your brain automatically goes back to that thought, back down that familiar trench, thereby deepening the trench. It will take time before new pathways are built. Here are four steps to success.

Four Steps to Building New Pathways

1. Identify your most frequent thought patterns. You can do this for every area of your life, but we're specifically focusing on those thoughts that affect your parenting and family. Therefore, pay close attention to the thoughts you have about your child, his behavior, your spouse or partner, your marriage, and yourself as a parent.

2. Jot down your most prevalent negative thoughts and challenge them. Then, write correctives to these thoughts. For example, if you have the recurring thought, *This kid is always pitching some kind of fit*, challenge that thought. Think, *STOP! Is she really always pitching a fit?* Then establish a corrective (and more compassionate) thought: *My child is really having a hard time with her emotions and needs my help.*

3. Work on stopping your negative thought mid-thought *every single time* and thinking the corrective thought instead. The more you repeat the corrective thought, the more that neural pathway gets reinforced, and eventually the corrective thought will be your automatic thought.

4. Enlist accountability. Since the two of you are going through this process together, hold each other accountable. Ask, "How are you doing with your thoughts today?" "What are you struggling with?" "How can I help?" Offer support and accept support.

Give yourself grace through this process. Know that you are taking a big step toward your happiness and your family's happiness, and give yourself a pat on the back for doing so. Realize that it will take time, and there will be good days and harder days. Keep going, turn to your partner for support, stay accountable, and keep a record of your progress in your journal. Celebrate your victories. If you notice that your typical negative thought didn't occur today, tell your partner about it and jot down a milestone in your journal. This is big news! Your new pathway is well under way.

You have done amazing self-work already. I commend you for taking these important steps for your family's well-being.

So far, you and your partner have looked at your pasts and how the events of your pasts have shaped who you each are today, asked yourselves some difficult questions, rewritten your stories to be more conducive to the people you want to become for your family, and are working hard on building those new neural pathways in your brains.

You have two more things to tackle in this self-work section, and then you're going to take your improved selves and unite into one unstoppable team. Next, we are going to talk about disciplining yourself before you attempt to discipline your kids, as well as identifying and deactivating your triggers. Thus far, you've been changing your perceptions and your thoughts. Now it's time to confront your actions.

Discipline Yourself First

During the times I have struggled the most in my parenting journey, an honest look has always revealed that I was the one off course, and my children were simply following their leader. When my patience was thin, or my words were unkind, this was reflected back to me in the behavior of my sons.

I recall one of the most trying times when my children were ages four and two. The peaceful home I had been knitting together seemed to be falling apart at the seams. My oldest was being slightly "mouthy," and my youngest was hitting and quite aggressive. I felt like a complete failure, and I just couldn't understand why they were behaving so poorly.

One night after I, at long last, had gotten my little ones to sleep, I sat there staring at my two-year-old's sweet, angelic face (the same one that had bitten his brother earlier), and I had an epiphany. I had been dealing with quite a bit of stress. My anxiety level was high, I was sleep deprived, and I bungled. I realized I wasn't actually being the mother I wanted to be at all. I had become short-tempered. I was going through the motions of positive parenting, such as taking my little biter to time-in rather than punishing him, and working on problem-solving and communication skills with my back-talker (we'll take a closer look at those techniques later in the book), but the truth is that I wasn't handling my own emotions—or behavior—very well. I was, to be quite honest, being mouthy and aggressive. I wasn't biting people, of course, but my tone was aggressive, and my emotional state had left me irritable and fatigued.

Aha! My children weren't being defiant. *They were being me.* I made a promise that night to make changes. I would consciously watch my tone, speak respectfully, keep my mood in check, and behave how I wanted them to behave.

In a very short time, things improved. We were playing more and connecting more. As I watched my tone and spoke respectfully, guess what? They started watching theirs and speaking respectfully, too. The peace returned to my home because I changed *my* behavior, not because I demanded that they change theirs.

That is how I learned a somewhat inconvenient truth: If I expect my children to be kind, gentle, compassionate, and respectful, I must be kind, gentle, compassionate, and respectful. Children do not listen to the instruction of hypocrites; it is your actions that guide their actions, not your lectures or your punishment. Words carry messages only to the ears, but actions speak to the heart. You see, you can read every positive parenting article there

> *To effectively discipline your children, you must first discipline yourself*

is and follow the advice to a T, but if you aren't controlling your own behavior, you can hardly expect your little ones to control theirs. Therefore, **to effectively discipline your children, you must first discipline yourself**.

I say it is an inconvenient truth because this requires some work for many of us who are used to the old "do as I say, not as I do" approach. Once you realize the power of modeling, you can no longer (with any integrity, at least) behave in unfavorable ways and then punish your child for following in your footsteps. This may require you to break your own negative behavior patterns, such as yelling when you're frustrated, smacking when you're angry, and any other habit you don't want your child to pick up.

The truth is that we really must be what we want them to be, and this often challenges us to grow up emotionally. Many of us are still stuck in childhood because we never learned how to effectively handle our emotions; we merely learned to stuff them away for fear of punishment, or to unleash them on those who had no authority over us. If we don't learn how to manage our emotions now, we can't teach our children how to manage theirs, and unfortunately they will have to bear the brunt of a harshness that they do not deserve. This disastrous behavior will trickle down through generations until someone takes a stand. Let that someone be you so that your children will not have to carry the weight of emotional instability.

Identifying Triggers

Somewhere along your journey, you've gotten armed with emotional triggers. It's okay; it happens to all of us. They are survival responses that got coded in your brain way back when. The important thing to remember is that triggers may explain your emotional outbursts, but they do not excuse them. It's time to take the responsibility for them now so that your family doesn't have the burden of tiptoeing around triggers they had no part in arming.

Maybe you don't yet know what your triggers are in regard to parenting. Maybe your child isn't even born yet. How lucky for that child that you are equipping yourself with this information now so that when an alarm does get tripped—and it will—you'll be ready. You've undoubtedly heard about how children can "push your buttons." The thing is, they're *your* buttons—your responsibility.

Now, let's identify your triggers. Think back to a time when you felt a strong negative emotion toward your child. Once you recall this particular moment, notice when your mood shifted. Triggers are something very specific, so it may take some time to tease out. Your children fighting, for example, isn't a trigger. That's a circumstance. The key is what happens inside your mind and body when your children fight and why. Let's take a look at how one might break down the scenario of children fighting to discover the real trigger, which, in this instance, is disrespect:

When my children fight, I hear disrespect. Disrespect makes me feel uncomfortable. I get this nervous feeling in the pit of my stomach and I begin to feel agitated. Why does disrespect cause me to have these feelings? What was I taught about disrespect as a child? What happened to me when my parent perceived I was being disrespectful? When my parent thought I was disrespectful, I got physically punished. So, I perceive that my children are disrespectful when they fight, and disrespect is something that must be punished. Now I see why my alarm is getting tripped, and perhaps the feelings of fear I felt as a child are being brought back to the surface. My brain is signaling that I must take action now to make it stop because these feelings are terribly uncomfortable for me. Once my alarm is tripped, I'm being flooded with hormones that increase my agitation and make me feel strong and aggressive, and I feel the need to release this horrible tension in my body, so I yell.

Notice that the children fighting actually has little to do with your reaction. That circumstance merely sets off a chain reaction. The fuse is lit. What you have to do is learn how to put out the fuse before it goes *boom*.

There is a space between every action and reaction. When you harness that space and consciously expand it, you can use that "breathing room" to put out the fuse. There are a lot of techniques and methods you can use to calm yourself down, but until you master that space, you won't have time to apply your techniques.

Awareness harnesses the space, and compassion puts out the fuse. Be aware of what is going on in your body and mind when the negative feelings first begin to surface. Take a deep breath, place your hand on your forehead or over your heart, and repeat to yourself, "I have a choice in this space." Now you are aware of your choice to let the fuse burn or to extinguish it.

Let compassion in. "We are okay; this is not an emergency." "I am calm and capable of handling this." "My child needs my help right now." This may sound like a very simple step, but it is very effective if you do it repeatedly, every single time you are triggered. These compassionate thoughts will signal your brain to calm down, and then you can use any of the following techniques to further soothe yourself so that you can respond to your child in a thoughtful and constructive way.

Calm-Down Techniques

1. Deep breaths in for a count of 4, hold for a count of 7, release for a count of 8. Repeat 4 times.
2. Be active. Do jumping jacks or push-ups, or jog around your living room.
3. Repeat an affirmation such as "I am a peaceful person."
4. Jot down something you're grateful for. Your brain can't easily focus on both positive and negative stimuli at the same time, so by intentionally focusing on something positive, you diminish the negative.
5. Use EFT (emotional freedom techniques), which is an emotional or psychological acupressure technique. You can find many how-to videos online. Try this: As you consciously expand the space between action and

reaction, use your thumb to apply pressure at the crease of your wrist on the little-finger side. This acupressure point relieves tension.

6. Look at a baby picture of your child. When you are locked in a power struggle with a spirited child, for example, looking at her baby picture will bring back tender feelings of adoration.

7. Call your partner or a friend whom you've enlisted to hold you accountable.

8. Get some fresh air. Step outside. Go for a short walk.

9. Close your eyes and imagine you are in peaceful surroundings or one of your favorite places.

10. Pick up this book and read a few paragraphs.

You may be thinking, *How am I supposed to do all of that when my kid is having a tantrum or we need to leave and she won't get her shoes on again?* This entire process can take less than two minutes, and believe me, it's so much better than two minutes spent yelling and making things worse. Plus, you're modeling for your child an important skill: self-regulation.

This is a huge milestone and an important key to positive parenting. It can be tempting to skip this step, but I'm being completely up front with you when I say it won't do you any good to know how to positively discipline your child unless you can effectively and positively discipline yourself, because your child will not take advice from someone who doesn't practice what he or she preaches. Put the work in now and you will not only be a good example for your child, but this skill will prove useful in all relationships throughout your life.

Discussion Questions

1. As a child, did you feel that what you had to say was important? Did you feel that your feelings and ideas mattered?
2. What were your parents' reactions when you showed intense emotions, such as fear, frustration, or anger? Were you comforted or punished?
3. How was your parents' relationship with each other? What did you determine about marriage and relationships from them?
4. What negative thoughts play on repeat in your mind? How do they make you feel? Are they true?
5. What corrective thoughts can take the place of your recurring negative thoughts?
6. What are the behaviors that you display that you don't want your child to pick up?
7. Which of your child's behaviors do you struggle with that have been learned from your own behavior? Do you ever punish your child for behaving like you? Is that fair?
8. How will you harness that space between emotion and response? List at least two steps you will take.

Once you've answered these questions, talk over your answers with your partner or a close friend. All of this communication is bringing you and your partner closer together, and that's good, because you're getting ready to unite your newly conscious selves into a team that your children will be thankful for the rest of their lives.

Putting It into Practice

This chapter's advice on self-work takes a lot of dedication. But it will be well worth the effort. The following outline will help you put this advice into practice.

Own Your Story

1. Review your story. Take an honest look at your past and think about how it has shaped you.
2. Express gratitude. Whatever happened, you're here now. You're strong and capable of positive change.
3. Notice the blame you place on others. Do you blame your mother for your anger, or an ex for your trust issues? When you own your behavior instead of blaming others, you are free to change.
4. Ask yourself what will happen to you and your relationships if you continue down the path you are on.
5. Rewrite your story. Shed a positive light where you can. Write yourself to be the hero of your life story.
6. Envision your best future. Imagine that you have succeeded at accomplishing all of your life goals. Write what you have accomplished and how you feel about the realization that you have made your dreams reality.

Change Your Thought Patterns

1. Identify your most frequent thought patterns. Pay particular attention to any negative thoughts about your children or your partner.
2. Enlist accountability. Having a listening partner to share your wins with is helpful. Ideally, your partner and you will be working on this together and will be accountable to each other.
3. Jot down your most prevalent negative thoughts and challenge them. Then, write correctives to these thoughts. Example: (Negative thought) *I can't believe he hit his sister. He is so mean. Where did I go wrong with him?* (Interruption) *Stop. That's not helpful.* (Challenge) *He isn't really a mean person. He picked me a handful of flowers earlier.*
4. Work on stopping your negative thought mid-thought *every single time* and thinking the corrective thought instead. The more you repeat the corrective thought, the more that neural pathway gets reinforced, and eventually the corrective thought will be your automatic thought. *He's developing normally and needs my help with managing his emotions right now.*

Practice Self-Discipline

1. Keep a journal of your outbursts and times when you didn't show good control of your behavior. This journal will help you identify your biggest triggers.

2. Practice harnessing that space between action and
   reaction by placing your hand over your heart or
   pressing your "third eye" acupressure point (the
   indentation at the bridge of the nose, between the
   eyebrows) and taking a few deep breaths. Choose a
   mantra such as "This is not an emergency" or "I am
   calm and capable of handling this" and repeat it as you
   take your breaths.

3

United We Stand

Coming together is a beginning; keeping together
is progress; working together is success.

—Henry Ford

HOPEFULLY YOU AND your partner have learned a lot about yourselves in chapter 2. That's good, because the first step in creating a strong relationship is creating a strong self. Now it's time to bring your differences to the table and sort them out.

Differences in marriage or a relationship are often seen as something to overcome, but this is not necessarily true. The differences can serve a great purpose, helping you learn and grow. The goal is not to overcome your differences but to reconcile them. John Gottman, founder of the Gottman Institute and author of many books on love, marriage, and relationships, says, "I believe we grow in our relationships by reconciling our differences. That's how we become more loving people and truly experience the fruits of marriage."[9]

Many disconnected couples stay stuck in their patterns of

communication and disputes and fail to do the work necessary to have a truly healthy relationship. It stands to reason, however, that in order to build a connected family, couples must take the initiative to reconcile their differences regarding parenting and family ideals. Disconnected parents have an impact on children and influence the beliefs children develop about what relationships look like. In this chapter, you will work on providing a good example relationship for your children to follow. What a beautiful gift to give them!

Bringing two people from different families together to form a new family rarely comes without stumbling blocks. The differences in how you each were raised, and thus how your home environment shaped you, are what we want to confront today. It is likely you two have different beliefs about child-rearing and your role as parents that you noted in the previous chapters. Couples rarely talk about these differences before having children because it simply doesn't occur to them. So, when the child enters the toddler stage and parenting styles begin to clash, problems often arise. You may have found this already to be true in your relationship. If so, that's okay. The fact that you are willing to go through this book together speaks volumes about your commitment. You can reconcile your differences and come to an agreement about how you want to raise your child as well as work to get your individual needs met in the relationship so that you each feel emotionally fulfilled.

Is one of you considered the "strict" parent and the other the "lenient" one? Often the strict parent becomes stricter to compensate for the perceived leniency of the other parent, while the lenient parent does the same, becoming too permissive. I'm guessing that one or both of you may have perceived positive parenting as too lenient before you understood the truth of the philosophy, and perhaps that has caused some tension in the relationship. Now that you both are on the same page with what positive parenting means, let's get to an agreement on how you now view your individual roles and how you feel you should parent your child.

Before we begin the process of literally laying it on the table, I want to add that your relationship, how you handle conflicts, how you treat each other, your affection or lack thereof, and the way you interact are all setting the tone in your home. During this process, respect and honor where each other came from and offer support and encouragement to your partner.

Ready? I would like for each of you to write down the answers to the following questions on strips of paper. Don't tell your partner what you're writing. It's important that you bring your honest opinion to the discussion.

1. I feel that my partner is a good parent because _____
   _____.

2. I feel that my role as a parent is to _____
   _____.

3. After reading this book up to this point, I feel that
   positive parenting is _____
   _____.

4. My parents were _____
   _____
   and I feel that was _____.

5. Discipline means _____

_____ .

6. It's most important to me for my child to be _____

_____ .

7. My goal in raising my child is _____

_____ .

Now, it's time to lay your answers on the table, one at a time. Start with the positive "I feel my partner is a good parent because _____" and lay your strip on the table. Ask your partner to do the same. Discuss what you've each written. Do the same for the remaining questions in numerical order.

Your entire relationship is not simply based on being Mom and Dad. You are individuals with a lot of roles other than that of parent. We are all juggling many hats. One of the most important, in addition to being a parent, is your role as partner. Recall when it was just the two of you—before your little blessing (or blessings) was born. There was a time before middle-of-the-night feedings and carpools when you were each other's world. **This family began with the two of you and your love for one another.** That love can get swept under the rug along with the Cheerios and dog fur if you aren't intentional about keeping the spark alive.

This family began with the two of you and your love for one another.

Where we focus our attention and intention is the direction in which our lives go. Over the years, as new, exhilarating love becomes familiar and comfortable love, we start to notice differences we didn't notice before. We can begin to focus on our partner's "character flaws" or "annoying" traits and completely miss the awesomeness of the person we are with. When we focus on flaws and annoyances, we are making a choice to do so. The other option, of course, is to see all of the wonderful things about him and focus on the light and love he brings to our life.

I've found that focusing on what I perceive to be a flaw in someone else is not only haughty, but it destroys my joy and causes disconnection. I have no shortage of negative traits, I'm sure, yet my husband always, without fail, sees the best in me. His continued faith in my innate goodness has been a tremendous blessing in my life, one that I hope to return to him and to my children.

Just as we focused on reconciling differences in regard to parenting earlier, let us focus on reconciling relational differences. In the same fashion as before, write your answers on strips of paper and then lay them on the table for discussion one at a time.

Note: If you feel that your disconnection is too great or that your relationship is unhealthy, please seek professional advice.

What I love most about you is _____.

I feel that my role as a husband/wife/partner is _____.

What I need out of this relationship most is _____.

In 20 years, I hope we are _____.

Now each of you write a list of your partner's positive traits. List as many as you can think of, and share them with each other to finish up this exercise.

The Connected Couple

I was a seventeen-year-old kid when I met my husband in a high school art class, which was lucky because he was good at art and I was not. Even luckier was that he ended up being more than I ever dreamed of, and he fell in love with me that year. I am a year and a half older than he is, which means I graduated the year we fell in love, and then I had to wait two years for him to graduate. (Time didn't move as quickly back in the 1990s as it does today. Does anyone at all have an explanation for that?)

At long last, he did escape high school, and then off we went to college. We dated for six years before we married. We then moved into a three-room apartment and juggled jobs, our final college classes, bills, and the transition to responsible adulthood. We have truly had a blessed union, but it hasn't been without trials. Working opposite shifts for several years required us to work extra hard at maintaining a connection. Financial problems had to be dealt with and other typical problems arose from time to time.

Through all of that, here we are in our twentieth year of happy coupledom. Sincerely, I have the honor and privilege of saying that I love him more today. He has been my someone, the one I can always count on to see my light and reflect it back to me when I'm in darkness. He's the one I can trust wholeheartedly. Our connected family was built upon first having a connected relationship, and so I'd like to take this time to offer fifteen simple tips I've learned over the past twenty years to foster a healthy union.

1. Fill up emotional tanks

Each man, woman, and child has an emotional tank that needs filling. Like the gas tank in your car, when the emotional tank gets low, the relationship starts to sputter. On an empty tank, it may well break down altogether. To keep your partner's tank on full:

- Be attuned to her emotions. Recognize when she is feeling happy, sad, worried, excited, frustrated, etc.
- Make daily emotional deposits. These are words of encouragement or loving gestures. A sweet text, a back rub, a compliment—these deposits keep the tank from getting too low.
- Listen to dreams, hopes, ideas, and desires. You are a team, and it should be your goal to help each other fulfill life's dreams.

2. Focus on the positives

You wish he'd do the dishes. He wishes you'd have more sex. Focusing on what you're not getting is a buzzkill. Focus instead on your partner's positive qualities and make it a point to express out loud your appreciation and admiration. It's okay to constructively discuss things you would like, such as washed dishes and sex, but have a polite and honest conversation about it rather than stewing on it. Come to an agreement and get back to admiring. Remember, what you focus on grows. It's, like, a universal law or something. Focus on the good.

When we see the best in others, we bring out the best in them, and in ourselves as well. We all need at least one person who sees the best in us and believes the best of us. Positive parents are that someone for their children, and in connected families, partners are that someone for each other. Look for the good in your partner with intention. You can even write down the good points you want to focus on and remind yourself of those points daily. This is especially helpful if you've been looking at the negative aspects for a long time. Refer back to how to change your thought patterns in chapter 2 for an overview on challenging and changing negative thoughts. Seeing the positive in your partner is a great start, but it needs to be spoken out loud. Use the power of your words to build up your loved ones.

3. Argue constructively

Conflict is inevitable, but connected couples set ground rules for solving disputes.

- If you are too wound up to fight fairly, agree to take a cool-off and come back to the issue later.
- Don't use your knowledge of your partner's insecurities or sensitivities to hurt him or her.
- Own your feelings and state them without laying blame on the other person.
- When disagreements arise, rather than insisting on get-

ting your way, look for common ground and work toward a solution.

- When you are tackling a problem, don't attack or criticize your partner. This is great advice in the parent-child relationship as well. State your feelings by expressing a positive need. Use "I" statements instead of "you" statements. For example, "I'm feeling a little cooped up. I would like it if we could drop the kids off and go on a date," instead of "You never take me anywhere!"
- Listen to hear, not just to respond. Make a point to understand your partner's argument and not simply to get your side heard.
- Violence is never an option. Refrain from violent language and actions at all times.

4. Treat each other with respect

Share in the power and the decision making. Treat each other as equals and honor the human being you're committed to. Mutual respect is a cornerstone of connected couples. In respectful relationships, partners not only refrain from negative actions (avoiding, ignoring, or insulting) but engage in positive actions (being courteous, considerate, and kind). Respectful partners learn to accept, and even appreciate, differences.

5. Be flirtatious

Don't stop trying to woo your partner. Just because you've made "the catch" doesn't mean it's wise to now ignore the fish you were after. My in-laws are a terrific example of this. They've been married for many, many years, and they're still playful and flirtatious with each other. My husband followed their example and brought that to our relationship as well. Wink across the table, make an "I just wanted to say I love you" call, wear something special, touch affectionately, have little inside jokes, and kiss often.

6. Give each other space

Connected couples don't have to be in each other's faces all the time to stay connected. It's healthy for each of you to have your own hobbies and interests as well, as long as they aren't detrimental to the family. While shared interests and hobbies are good for connection as well, everyone needs time alone to just be. Respect and honor that need.

7. Be intimate

Intimacy can fall by the wayside in the early days of parenthood if we aren't intentional, but keeping intimacy alive both in and out of the bedroom is important in a connected relationship. Intimacy is more than sex; it's an emotional closeness. It's being able to let your guard down and be who you are, to express your wide range of emotions and thoughts and know that you will be accepted and loved.

Being sexually intimate is also an important part of a connected relationship. It's an emotional need, even more so for most men, and it's not to be used as a weapon. Withholding in an attempt to punish or manipulate him (or her) is very disrespectful and causes resentment to build up, which will undoubtedly lead to disconnection.

8. Have fun together

Keep regular date nights, even if this is microwaved chicken nuggets in the living room after the kids go to bed. Mark it on the calendar and protect this time slot, because it's very important for connected couples. Make it a point to laugh together, which decreases stress and increases emotional health. Every now and then, do something spontaneous. Trying new things together will build your emotional bond.

9. Show appreciation

We can fall into the habit of assuming that our partner knows we are appreciative. Even if this is true, it's always nice to be reminded that we are appreciated. Whether you've been together a month or two decades, be mindful not to take your partner for granted. Express gratitude for your partner's efforts on a daily basis, and be sure to express *why* you are grateful. "Thank you for helping me with the dishes. Now I have some time to relax."

Let your partner know how important he or she is in your goals and pursuits in life. When he supports your endeavor in positive parenting, tell him how much that means to you. When she backs your work goals, thank her. We need to feel like we are more than paycheck earners or housekeepers and that we are making a significant and appreciated contribution to the lives of our loved ones.

10. Be affectionate

Affection is another emotional need that can fall off the radar without mindful intention. Showing affection to your partner boosts oxytocin and reduces stress. Just as we do not withhold affection from a child whose behavior we may not like, we are not to withhold affection from our partners if they are not doing our bidding. Love and affection is not a carrot to be dangled in front of those we love; it is a lifeline in a loving and connected relationship.

11. Be trustworthy

Building trust is essential in all connected relationships. I've included an entire chapter on building trust with your child (chapter 5), and let's not neglect to build and honor trust with our partners as well.

- Be honest. Do not withhold information or mask the truth.
- Keep your word. Don't fall short on your promises to each other.
- Be faithful to your partner. What may seem like innocent flirting with another person is deceitful and a slippery slope that should be avoided.
- Keep confidences. Don't share your partner's secrets or speak negatively behind his or her back.

12. Curb criticism

Criticism erodes self-esteem, trust, and connection. This is true for your partner and your children. Psychologist John Gottman is world renowned for his work on marital stability and divorce prediction and has spent the past forty years conducting breakthrough research with thousands of couples. He calls criticism one of the "four horsemen" of the demise of a relationship, likening it to the apocalyptic end foretold in the New Testament. In other words, criticism is one of the four things that will bring an end to a relationship. He notes that criticism is different from voicing a complaint or offering a critique, stating that criticism makes your partner feel assaulted, rejected, and hurt. He says that the antidote to criticism is "blameless complaints," in which you use "I" statements and express a positive need.[10] This is discussed more in the next chapter.

13. Share leadership

While it is perfectly fine to agree to delegate tasks, things such as running the home and raising the children aren't just one partner's job. Everything is a collaborative effort.

14. Be proactive when it comes to common relationship problems

Typical issues that come between partners are differences in child-rearing, money worries, poor communication, and problems with shared leadership. Therefore, discuss a plan of action for such issues before they arise so that you will not be caught off guard. Most are addressed in this book.

15. Communicate effectively

Just as communicating in a clear and supportive way is essential with our kids, it's also essential between partners. Learning effective communication skills brings us deeper understanding of our loved ones and leads to a more fulfilling relationship. Effective communication is discussed in detail in the next chapter.

These tips may seem like a no-brainer, but with the hustle and bustle of our over-scheduled, busy lives, connection often gets pushed down the list as we have less and less quality time to spend together. Without intention, kindness happens but only in short moments of passing, generosity diminishes because we simply feel there is little left to give, and attention is divided rather than devoted. Commit to maintaining your connection with each other and you'll be one step closer to your dream of a connected family.

Discussion Questions

1. Is there a harmful or negative pattern in your relationship that needs to be addressed?
2. Is your attention focused on the positive or negative traits of the people in your life?
3. Will you commit to looking for and pointing out the goodness of those you love?
4. Will you commit to reconciling your differences for the sake of building a connected family?

Share the answers to the following questions with your partner.

5. What makes me feel loved?
6. What makes me feel appreciated?
7. Is there anything lacking in the relationship that I would like to resolve?

Putting It into Practice

For easy review, here's a quick overview of my fifteen tips to foster a healthy union.

1. Fill up emotional tanks.
2. Focus on the positives.
3. Argue constructively.
4. Treat each other with respect.
5. Be flirtatious.
6. Give each other space.
7. Be intimate.
8. Have fun together.
9. Show appreciation.
10. Be affectionate.
11. Be trustworthy.
12. Curb criticism.
13. Share leadership.
14. Be proactive when it comes to common relationship problems.
15. Communicate effectively.

To put building a healthy union into practice even further, do the following exercises:

1. Choose a few of your partner's traits that you love. Focus on those traits in the days to come; be intentional about noticing them and verbally expressing your appreciation to your partner. The more you focus on his or her positive traits, the more positive feelings will flourish.

2. Set aside a time slot a few nights a week to turn off all distractions and just hold each other. Whether it's ten focused minutes on the couch for my co-sleepers out there or a two-hour lockdown in the boudoir (you lucky duck), it's sure to enhance your connection.

3. Practice active listening with your partner. Allow him to vent to you about whatever he needs to. The listener's job is to simply listen attentively, not to offer advice or judgments. Take turns.

4. Eye gazing is a great connection exercise. Sit comfortably facing each other. Touch each other lightly as you feel comfortable. Clear your minds and gaze into each other's eyes. Maintain eye contact for three to five minutes.

4

Communicating Effectively

Give me the gift of a listening heart.
—King Solomon

IT CAN BE challenging when two people with different back-grounds and perspectives unite, yet learning to communicate effectively is essential for a connected family. As previously dis-cussed, each of you learned how to communicate in childhood. How your parents communicated with each other and with you set the example for what communication is supposed to be. If you learned negative communication skills growing up, it can be challenging to break out of old patterns, but if we've learned anything so far in this book, it's that we are capable of change.

The truth is that many of us have learned to offer only con-ditional love, and we convey this in our communication, both verbally and nonverbally. We often take on an "I'll scratch your back if you scratch mine" attitude. Our own behavior is usually dependent on the behavior of those around us, but we can take a higher road. **We can choose to be loving even if we aren't feeling loved.**

We can choose to be warm when others are being cold. We can choose to be calm in the face of anger and kind in response to unkindness. We can be the ones to bring light into the darkness.

We can choose to be loving even if we aren't feeling loved.

Effective communication is more than just an exchange of information. It helps us to understand our partners and our children better. It helps us to connect, solve problems, and convey emotions. Understanding the emotion behind the exchange of information is really what effective communication is all about; it's tuning in to our partners (and others) to hear the meaning behind the words. That brings us a deeper understanding of the ones we share our lives with and leads to more fulfilling relationships overall.

We all have a great need to feel heard and understood, and yet many of us aren't good at conveying what we really want to say. We may use an off-putting tone in a moment of frustration, or we may try to hide our feelings, causing a lack of communication, which is confusing and frustrating for our loved ones. Still others only want to get their own needs met and aren't concerned with reciprocating, while some get immediately defensive and wall themselves off at the mention of certain subjects or emotions. These are barriers that we must break through for the sake of our families. It's time to learn healthier communication patterns so you can build lasting bonds with one another.

Do any of these negative communication signs ring true for either of you?

- You invalidate emotions. "It's not that big a deal! You're overreacting!"
- You clam up when strong emotions are present. "I'm fine. I don't want to talk about it."
- You yell or say hurtful things during conflict.
- You keep all of your emotions and thoughts bottled up and then explode all at once.
- You overgeneralize. "You *always* leave your dirty clothes on the floor." "You *never* take me out anywhere." "You forget this *all the time*."
- You lay blame on your partner.
- You criticize or put down your partner.

Of those that ring true, how many were demonstrated in your home when you were a child? The communication patterns we learned in childhood can be rewired with mindfulness. You can learn to communicate effectively and in a way that deepens your relationship. For that reason, it's good to set some ground rules regarding communication in your family.

Examples:

- We will not discuss things when we are angry; we will not go to bed angry.
- We will use "I" statements and not lay blame.
- We will look for win-win solutions.

"I" Before "You" Will Help You Get Through

Learning how to replace "you" statements with "I" statements will be beneficial in all of your relationships. Using "I" statements is assertive but not aggressive—it is a way to communicate what you need without attacking your loved one. The way you start a discussion often determines how the discussion will go, so try to start on a positive note, stating your feelings without blaming the other person. For example, "You make me furious when you don't get home on time" isn't a good way to begin a healthy conversation. Just like children, when we feel attacked, our defenses kick in, and we are no longer receptive to what the other person is saying. Instead, try, "I feel worried when you are late, and I begin to get overwhelmed." Typically, starting a conversation with "I feel _____ when/because _____" will help your partner be more receptive to whatever you have to say.

A Win-Win Is a Good Place to Begin

Look for win-win solutions to problems. This is another relationship skill that you will carry over into your parent-child relationship. Win-win is about being cooperative rather than competitive. According to Stephen R. Covey, author of *The 7 Habits of Highly Effective People*, "Win-win is a frame of mind and heart that constantly seeks mutual benefit in all interactions." It means looking for a solution that is responsive to the concerns of everyone. To accomplish this, each person must discuss in depth his or her needs and wants surrounding an issue and brainstorm ways both people can get those needs met.

While this is a straightforward process, it isn't always easy to achieve. Many arguments involve each person trying to convince the other why he or she is right. To find a win-win solution, each person must be open to the desires of the other's heart.

The five-step process of reaching a win-win is as follows:

1. Separate the person from the problem. You may not like your partner's stance on discipline, but you love your partner. This may sound rather obvious when there is no conflict, but when a conflict arises and both sides are locked in a tug-of-war, it becomes quite easy to let your negative feelings regarding the problem spill over onto the person. Just as we disengage from a power struggle with our child by looking behind the behavior to the human being and how that person is being motivated to behave in such a way, we must learn to look behind the problems that arise with our partners to see the beliefs and emotions motivating the conflict.

2. Assess beliefs, emotions, and concerns. Remember that each person has her own unique story that has formed her current beliefs. These differences in beliefs can present challenges, particularly in parenting, but through respectful dialogue and empathetic listening, you will understand the heart behind the viewpoint and the story behind the position. Through truly seeking to understand the other's point of view rather than simply trying to get yours across, you open up new possibilities.

3. Explore, invent, and rethink options. In this brainstorming phase, remain honest and open to your partner's ideas. At the same time, don't be shy about saying a particular idea doesn't work for you.

4. Settle on a solution you both feel good about. If you're having trouble, aim to meet key concerns. As a quick example, Janet and Dan are in conflict over whether or not to spank their kids. Janet's key concern is the negative effects on child development. Dan's key concern is being permissive and not disciplining at all. The couple settles on a discipline plan that doesn't involve spanking but assures that their child isn't getting by with misbehavior. Both key concerns have been addressed.

5. Give the solution a fair chance. Once a solution is reached, try it out for a few weeks. If one person feels it isn't working well and is unhappy with the solution, go back to step 2.

To Assume Makes One Fume

It's always better to ask than to assume. Assumptions about what your partner is thinking or feeling can lead to unnecessary anger and bitterness. Let's say Jenny bought a new outfit for her date night with her husband, John. John does not comment on how lovely she looks. He may very well think she looks lovely, but maybe he assumes she already knows that. Meanwhile, she's assuming that he either doesn't notice her effort or doesn't like how she looks, or maybe even that he disapproves of the money she spent on the outfit. Her feelings of hurt, concern, and defensiveness fester throughout the entire date. This can be avoided, of course, by John telling her she looks lovely, and by Jenny simply asking, "How do I look?"

Let's say Anna always gets up with the baby in the middle of the night. Resentment builds as she assumes that Jeff feels it's her job to do so. Jeff, meanwhile, assumes that she wants to be the one to get up with the baby because she's never said otherwise. He'd be more than happy to get up if she'd only ask. Saying how you feel and checking in with your partner about his or her feelings is an essential part of a healthy relationship. If it doesn't come naturally to you at first, make a conscious effort. The payoff will make it worthwhile, and soon it will become a cherished way to stay connected.

Listen, Listen so There's No Division

Just because you're hearing your partner speaking doesn't mean you're listening. Focus your attention on the speaker. Maintain good eye contact and receptive body language. Nothing says *I don't care* like looking away and being distracted, or worse, rolling your eyes and crossing your arms and legs. Put down your phone and don't multitask with chores while you're having a conversation. Listen objectively, and try not to put words in your partner's mouth. Paraphrase to the speaker what you heard, just to make sure you haven't misconstrued anything.

Halt with the Finding Fault

Criticism is a conversation killer. Finding fault in your partner, laying blame, and pointing out everything he or she is doing wrong or could be doing differently isn't helpful at all. It's not your job to look at what your partner could do differently. It's your job to look at what *you* could do differently.

Drop It When It's Hot

As I mentioned in the Brain Science 101 section in chapter 1, the downstairs (primitive) brain is activated when you are angry. This makes it difficult to access your upstairs (logical) brain. This doesn't only happen to children. It's the reason we yell and then feel guilty later. We yell from our reactive, primitive brain, and then when we are able to think logically again, we realize we shouldn't have yelled. So, when the talk gets heated, take a break to calm yourself and wait until you feel the anger subside and you're able to think clearly and speak calmly. Refer to chapter 2 for calm-down techniques.

Communicating with Children

I've learned over the years that the way I communicate with my children determines how they respond to me. They often meet me with the same tone that I meet them with. In other words, I get what I give, and I want my children to learn that in a connected and loving relationship, communication is respectful and kind.

Positive communication is one of the most practical ways to build healthy relationships. Communication is not only the words we say, but the way we say them, our tone of voice, our nonverbal cues and behavior, and our written words. Making eye contact and giving full attention can communicate *you are important* just as much as saying those actual words, if not more so. Giving your child the silent treatment also gives him or her a message: "You do not deserve my attention and warmth right now." Thus, it isn't only the words that come out of our mouths that we must be mindful of, but all the ways in which we communicate.

Keep in mind what you already know to be true: The method of communication we tend to carry out in our lives is learned in childhood. This means you are teaching your child how to communicate with every interaction. You can give her a head start on healthy relationships by teaching her positive communication skills now.

Respect

It is a widely held misconception that we must speak harshly to children for them to listen. Parents often say, "My child won't listen unless I yell!" If that is the case, then I'm afraid that's what she's been taught to respond to. The unfortunate truth is that the more often you use yelling and harsh words or tones to "make your child listen," the more often you'll need to, because she will learn that she doesn't really need to act until you blow your top. Moreover, she'll learn that's how to communicate with others to get her way, so you may see her speaking in that same harsh or loud manner to a sibling or peers, or even to you.

Remember what I said earlier—you can be loving even when you aren't feeling loved. You can be warm when your child is being cold. You can be calm when he's being angry and kind when he's being unkind. You are the adult. You are the model. It is possible to get your point across without the booming authoritarian voice you may have been used to hearing when you were growing up. Yelling and threats tend to shut kids down. It puts them on the defensive, activating their reactive lower brain. Being respectful doesn't give them the message that you aren't in charge. It tells them that they are respectable. That's something you want your child to believe about herself, isn't it?

Encouragement and Praise

There's been a lot written about praise. Alfie Kohn has done wonderful research on this topic, and I'm not going to attempt to detail his findings in this book, but certainly look him up if you want to delve more extensively into this topic. What I will do is provide a concise overview of what is generally held in the positive-parenting community as wise parenting.

Encouragement is good for children. It helps them to blossom and thrive. "I believe in you." "You can do this!" "Keep trying. I'm sure you'll figure it out." "You are doing great! Keep up the great work."

Praise is also good as long as it isn't empty praise given for the sole purpose of getting the child to perform for you. It is best when given as a sincere appreciation and acknowledgment of the child's efforts rather than a simple judgment of the outcome. "Thank you for picking up your toys. That was very helpful" offers the child something more than "Good job, Billy." "This history test was very challenging. You studied hard and put the effort in."

The point is that it is good for the child to (1) feel seen by you and know that you acknowledge and appreciate her, (2) be able to make her own judgments on the quality of her work and not learn to rely on everyone's approval to find satisfaction, and (3) understand that sometimes she will fail and sometimes she will succeed, and that trying is an opportunity to learn something new.

Conditional Communication

If you've ever had someone not speak to you when he's upset or purposefully turn his back when you enter the room, you know how this rejection stings. This is not an effective way to get a child to behave. In fact, giving your child the silent treatment or the cold shoulder is not a mature way to communicate and sets a rather poor example. This is conditional love. Friends, love is not a reward. Hugs, attention, affection, kind words—these are not rewards to be dangled in front of a child, only given when he performs to our liking and jerked away when he doesn't. These are a child's lifeline. They should be given without condition and without hesitation, always.

Body Language

Body language is part of communication and can constitute 50 percent or more of what we are communicating. You say a lot without speaking a word. Do you smile when your child enters the room? Do you sit up straight and make eye contact when she tells you about her day? You can be aggressive, attentive, bored, relaxed, open, and much more in your body language alone. If you want to communicate positively, then it makes sense to understand what kind of body language is positive. The following convey positive messages:

- leaning forward
- making eye contact
- ignoring distractions
- tilting your head slightly forward

- keeping your arms legs and arms open, not crossed
- making gentle gestures
- smiling
- holding a relaxed gaze
- nodding

Written Word

The written word has a way of reaching secret places in the heart where spoken words cannot go. Don't underestimate the value of a well-timed note of love and encouragement—in a lunch box, propped up at the dinner table, tucked into a book bag, or resting on your child's pillow. A "Mom and me" journal is also a great way to communicate in a way that may help your child feel safer about expressing thoughts and feelings to you. Private journaling is an effective way for your school-age or older child to work through thoughts and emotions.

Communication Styles

Communicate in a way that relates to the age and interest of the child. Following is an outline of communication styles through the stages of childhood.

Infants: 0–12 Months

Infants actively communicate with crying, sounds, and nonverbal cues, and how we interpret these cues is important in the development of secure attachment. Nonverbal cues include facial expressions such as smiles and grimaces, movements such as kicking legs, and gestures such as pointing, nodding, and shaking their heads. Babies also squeal, laugh, and babble to communicate with caregivers. To encourage infant communication:

- Talk and sing to your baby often.
- Respond quickly and warmly to cries.
- Read to her often. She may not understand what you're saying, but she will enjoy listening to your voice, and this helps her appreciate language early on.
- Copy her sounds and gestures. Hold a "conversation" with her by imitating her verbalizations and pausing for her to "answer."
- Use a warm, happy voice when talking to her.
- Show interest when your baby laughs, coos, and babbles. Look at her and respond to encourage this communication to continue.
- Mirror her facial expressions.
- Engage her listening skills by talking to her often throughout the day.

Toddlers: 12–36 Months

In addition to cries, sounds, and nonverbal cues, toddlers are beginning to use language to communicate. To encourage communication and language development in toddlers:

- Always show interest in and respond to attempts at communication. This shows that you value communicating with him and models good communication skills.

- Interpret your child's gestures. If he's pointing to his juice cup, say, "Oh, juice! You want juice!"
- Sportscast while your child plays. This develops grammar skills and helps with thought organization. "You're driving the train around the track. Here comes a tunnel! You went through the tunnel!"
- Encourage imaginative play. Children often express themselves more freely during pretend play. Join in their imaginative play with them.
- Eliminate negative responses like "Grass is not red" and "Trains don't go on roads" when your child is playing.
- Give your child a good vocabulary for emotions by labeling and talking about emotions often.
- Discuss the feelings and expressions of others. "Do you see how Nathan's hands are covering his ears? He doesn't like the loud noise." This teaches children to look for nonverbal cues and builds communication skills.
- Respect your child's feelings. It's important to acknowledge and respect his emotions even when you must correct the behavior.
- Connect words with actions. "I'm washing your toes!"
- Read with your child. Encourage him to point to what he sees and name it. Allow him to turn the pages.
- Make requests clear, age appropriate, and simple.

Preschoolers: 3–5 Years

Now they're talking! Preschoolers want to chat a lot to try out all their new skills. Establishing an atmosphere where your child is able to freely talk about her thoughts, feelings, and ideas is crucial. To encourage preschooler communication:

- Continue to join in her imaginative play and provide lots of opportunities for free play with you or with friends.
- Ask questions about her day, past events, or how she's feeling. Offer descriptive terms when needed.
- Encourage your child to express both positive and negative emotions and give her the tools she needs to express them appropriately.
- Read great classic literature aloud every day.
- Continue to talk through her emotions and teach her problem-solving skills.
- Preschoolers may ask "why" or "how" often. Don't dismiss these questions as unimportant. Do your best to answer them.
- Give your full attention when your preschooler wants to communicate with you. Engage in active listening, and summarize back to your child what you heard.
- Nod, smile, and be warm and affectionate with her. This helps her feel valued and encourages continued communication.
- Watch body language and behavior cues. Preschoolers still can't always verbalize what's wrong.
- Give reasons for your rules. "We hold hands in the parking lot so you won't get hit by a car." "You need to wear your helmet when you ride your bike to protect your head in case you fall off."
- Curb criticism and offer lots of encouragement.

School-Age Children: 5–12 Years

School-age children are beginning to view the world in more complex ways. They think more logically and are able to be more reflective. They also begin to ask challenging questions. To encourage school-age communication:

- Make an effort to spend quality time together in which there is ample opportunity for open conversation.
- Ask specific, rather than general, questions.
- Work together to solve conflicts. Ask your child for his input on how to solve the problem, and allow him to have some say in the rules and outcomes.
- Keep encouraging him to talk about his emotions, positive and negative.
- Don't interrupt your child. Allow him to finish before you thoughtfully respond. Children appreciate this as much as adults do!
- Avoid criticism.
- Show interest in your child's interests. Ask questions and be genuinely curious about the things he loves.

Discussion Questions

1. What communication patterns do you think you picked up as a child?
2. What standard of communication would you like to set for your children?
3. Did your parents communicate respectfully with you?

How has that affected how you communicate with your child?

4. Do you have a tendency toward conditional communication—withholding words and warmth when you are displeased?
5. Pay attention to your body language. What do you convey?
6. What specific improvements can you make in the way you communicate with your child?

Putting It into Practice

With a bit of practice, positive communication will become your natural way of communicating with your family. Remember to practice these following points:

- Use "I" statements. Rather than saying, "You never help out with the kids," try "I would appreciate more help with the kids." This doesn't put your partner on the defensive right away.
- Look for win-win solutions. Remember the five-step process outlined in the chapter: (1) Separate the problem from the person, (2) assess beliefs, emotions, and concerns, (3) explore, invent, and rethink options, (4) settle on a solution you both are happy with, and (5) give the solution a fair trial. Drop the assumptions. Assuming what your partner is thinking or feeling often causes ill feelings or resentment. It's best to just ask.
- Listen objectively. Our tendency is to be thinking up the best response to get our thoughts heard. Instead, learn to

listen attentively, making a point to really understand how your loved ones are feeling.

- Don't criticize your family members. Criticism tears down, and we are encouragers and life givers.
- Take a break if you're angry. Don't continue a discussion until you're calm.
- Speak respectfully to your partner and children. You get what you give.
- Offer encouragement and genuine praise.
- Don't withhold attention and affection in an attempt to discipline your child or get back at your partner. It's an immature way to communicate your feelings.
- Watch your body language. Use the open, attentive body language discussed in this chapter.
- Use the written word. Leave love notes on pillows and jokes in lunch boxes.

Try the following exercises to build communication skills.

Three-Minute Listening Challenge

You'll need four to eight index cards with a topic written on each. Divide the family into pairs, each made up of a speaker and a listener. The speaker blindly chooses a card and talks about the topic for three minutes. The listener cannot speak during this time. After three minutes, the listener must then summarize what the speaker has said without agreeing, disagreeing, or debating. Then the speaker and listener switch roles.

The benefit: Part of effective communication is learning to

listen and to understand, not just to respond. This exercise strengthens listening skills because the listener must accurately summarize what the speaker said, so he or she must truly pay attention, with empathy and intention.

Obstacle Course

Create an obstacle course with scattered furniture (chairs, cushions, etc.) and divide the family into pairs, with one wearing a blindfold. The sighted partner must guide the blindfolded person safely through the obstacle course to the other side of the room. The blindfolded person must use only his or her listening skills to avoid running into objects.

The benefit: This activity builds trust and listening skills.

Silent Acting

Two people will be having a conversation in this game, but only one is allowed to speak. Person A will speak his part while person B must communicate his lines in a nonverbal way.

Give each person a copy of this script:

A: Have you seen my notebook? I don't know where I left it.

B: Which notebook?

A: The blue one. I let you borrow it yesterday.

B: Is this it?

A: No. That one's red. It's the one you borrowed.

B: I did not!

A. Maybe it's under the couch. Will you look?

B: Sure. Give me a minute.

A: How long is this going to take?

B: Geez! You're so impatient. I hate when you're bossy.

A: Forget it. I'll find it myself.

B: Wait! Here it is! I found it!

Benefit: This exercise shows how we can communicate a lot without saying a word!

Now give person B a secret emotion, such as nervous, bored, or excited, to act out while communicating his lines. Have person A guess what emotion is affecting person B.

Bonus benefit: This exercise builds emotional intelligence by showing how our emotions can affect our behavior, and how that gets communicated to others even when we don't speak.

Notes of Appreciation

List three things that each family member has done recently that made you feel loved. Ask them to do the same. Write each list on a separate note for each person, then exchange notes and bask in feeling loved and appreciated. To make a daily habit of noticing the good, start an appreciation board. We use a dry-erase board. Encourage each family member to write one thing he or she appreciates on the board before bed, and watch as positive feelings flourish.

5

Building a
Foundation of Trust

Trust is the fruit of a relationship in which you
know you are loved. —William P. Young

CONNECTION AND TRUST are the foundation upon which your
relationship with your child will be built. This foundation of
connection is based on one of the core principles of positive
parenting: attachment. Lovingly and consistently meeting your
child's needs has a positive, long-lasting influence on brain development. Once a child feels assured that his needs will be met
by his caregiver, his brain is ready to learn. He is then free
to explore his world. Without secure attachment, however,
learning is hindered because the focus is on getting primary
needs met.

The benefits of a secure attachment are numerous and include better childhood and adult relationships, increased empathy, better emotional health, less anxiety, increased ability to
sustain attention, greater creativity, and a better ability to cope

with life's ups and downs. Research has shown
that a secure attachment is the best possible
foundation for healthy emotional, intellectual,
physical, and social development.

You can foster trust and connect with a child of any age

While it is best to begin in infancy, **you can
foster trust and connect with a child of any
age.** It's never too late to start.

Building Trust with Your Infant

From the very beginning, infants are learning to either trust or
not trust the world. Their view of the world is being shaped by
you, the caregiver. If you consistently meet the infant's basic
needs for food, love, and affection, she learns to trust. What's
more, children make a determination of their value based on
the messages they receive from you and other caregivers. Of
course, you want that message to be "You are valuable," which
is a message she'll take with her, rooted in her self-concept,
throughout her life. Indeed, a secure attachment is an invaluable gift to give your infant.

To build trust and connection with your infant:

- Get to know your infant's cues and respond to them
  promptly.
- Feed her at the first hunger cues, before she begins to cry,
  if possible. As you feed her, talk softly and make eye contact.
- Smile, talk, and interact frequently with your baby.
- Give plenty of hugs, kisses, snuggles, and skin-to-skin
  contact.

- Respond promptly to cries. Never allow your baby to cry it out alone. Nighttime parenting is exhausting but important. Infants need to be parented back to sleep. If they wake frequently and you need help, there are gentle ways to teach better sleep habits. Look up Elizabeth Pantley for gentle sleep solutions.

Building Trust with Your Toddler or Preschooler

Toddlerhood is the time when children develop a sense of self-awareness. Your toddler is now beginning to understand that he is independent and separate from others. He will need you to be his home base as he begins to explore further into his world.

Follow these guidelines for a trusting and secure relationship during these years:

- Practice what you preach. Even young children can see when you're not being authentic. Remember, the example you set is more important than the words you say.
- Listen to the little things now so he'll tell you the big things later. You may not be greatly interested in hearing about what happened at preschool or why a particular toy is so awesome, but show interest anyway. You're laying the foundation for respectful communication in these early years.
- Be honest. It's tempting to say that the park is closed when you're really just too busy to take him, but honesty is always the best policy. He's young, not unintelligent. Respect him enough to tell him the truth. You'd want the same, wouldn't you?

- Keep your promises. If you say you'll lie down with him at bedtime for an extra story tonight, make sure you follow through. Your word is important now because you want his word to be important later—so you teach the value of keeping your promises. Don't make any that you can't keep.
- Praise the process, not the result. You want to convey the message that trying is what counts, not getting it perfect. "You are working really hard on getting those puzzle pieces to fit!" This teaches the value of effort, and it builds connection when you take the time to stop and acknowledge your child.
- Schedules and routines are important. We'll talk more about this in chapter 6. These create a sense of safety for young children.

Building Trust in Middle Childhood

An enormous amount of change and growth occurs between early and middle childhood. Middle childhood is when the parts of the brain that mediate social learning and emotional regulation are primed. Your five- to twelve-year-old is showing more independence and more understanding about her place in the world, and she's starting to think about her future. Self-concept is still developing, and while she is more independent, her connection with you is still vital.

Here's how to keep the trust and connection going in middle childhood:

- Show interest in what interests your child. Join her in her world.

- Don't make hyperbolic threats; they only serve to discon-nect. Make sure she is aware of the rules and the outcome of broken rules. This completely eliminates the need to threaten. An example of a hyperbolic threat is, "If you don't pick up these toys right now, they're going in the trash!" This isn't going to elicit cooperation, and do you really want to throw them away?

- Don't overact. Keep your emotions in check and your re-sponses in line with the situation. Making mountains out of molehills will only result in you tiring yourself out climbing unnecessary mountains. Few things are really a crisis, and a few bad choices don't make bad people.

- Show faith. Let your child know that you have faith in her. This is crucial to her being able to have faith in herself.

- Keep confidences. If your daughter tells you a secret, keep it. Don't betray her trust by blurting her secret to another family member or friend, unless, of course, there is dan-ger. Children need someone they can trust, and you want that person to be you.

- Children this age care about the opinions of their peers. It's best not to correct your child in front of her peers, but rather pull her aside and whisper it in her ear, or save it for later if you can. It's embarrassing to be called out in front of your friends, and this may lead to mistrust and discon-nection.

- Connect by telling stories of your childhood. Children this age are interested in hearing about the time you went through something similar to what they are going through and how you handled it. This helps them to know you bet-ter, too.

Building Trust with Your Teen

Teens may look grown-up, but remember that their brain development is still under way until about their midtwenties. I highly recommend Dr. Dan Siegel's book *Brainstorm* if you have an adolescent. While this is a time to start letting go in many ways, you never have to let go of trust and connection.

Here are some tips for keeping trust and connection healthy and strong during the teen years.

- Keep an open line of communication. This is why it's important that you listened to those little things in toddlerhood and set an example of honesty and integrity in your speech through the years, and hopefully you made a habit long ago of listening without offering quick judgment.
- Convey trust. It's still important to show faith in your child. Letting him know you believe in him will boost his self-esteem, which could always use a boost during these years.
- Be respectful of his space and need for privacy.
- Respect his opinion and don't downplay his concerns. He needs you to set the example of the kind of listening and respect for others that fosters healthy relationships.

If you lay this foundation well in the early years, it will be much easier to build on it as the years go by. If, for whatever reason, the opportunity to build a secure connection was missed in the early years, simply start where you are and do the best you can. Store up a lot of grace—for yourself and for your child—to tap into in times of turbulence and trial. When breaks happen, reconnect as soon as possible. When trust is broken, seek to mend it. It will always be your responsibility as the adult to initiate the reconnection and repair. It is always the obligation of the more mature mind to reach out first and lead the way.

Discussion Questions

1. Do you feel that you had a strong connection with your own parents? Did you trust them? Do you feel they trusted you?
2. Can you perceive how that trust or mistrust, connection or disconnection you had with your own parents may be seeping into the relationship you currently have with your own child?
3. How do you plan to build trust and connection with your child starting now?

Putting It into Practice

Without a solid foundation of trust and connection, children will not follow their parents' guidance without force or the threat of force. Because positive parenting does not rely on force, but on cooperation that comes naturally through being connected and trusting one another, this will only work if you stay connected to your kids. Building trust builds connection. Here's an overview by stage for quick reference:

Ages 0–12 Months

- Learning your infant's cues is key to building trust. Infants communicate mostly through cries, and your infant will have different cries for different needs. By being attuned to your baby, you will learn her cries and cues. Respond promptly and warmly to build trust.
- Shower her with affection. Don't worry about spoiling her by holding or cuddling her too much.
- Boost cognitive development by smiling, singing, playing, laughing, and talking frequently.

Ages 1–5

- Provide consistency and familiarity through routines and rituals.
- Be a good listener. When your child wants to talk to you, even when it's about something you find completely uninteresting, act interested! We always want to send the message, "What matters to you matters to me."
- Do you best to live your values and ideals and to provide the best example you can for your child. He will be mimicking your actions more than listening to your lectures.
- Be an encourager. See the best in him and point it out. Offer genuine praise and appreciation. Constant criticism erodes trust, so avoid it as best you can.
- Keep your promises. To raise trustworthy children, model trustworthiness.

Ages 5–12

- Continue showing faith in your child's innate goodness and capabilities. Your belief in her is a powerful connector. Your faith is her guiding light.
- Threats break down trust. Rather than make threats, be assertive. Be clear in your boundaries and expectations. "When . . . then" statements are helpful for avoiding threats. For example, "When your homework is done, then you may watch television" instead of "If you don't get your homework done, *no* television for you tonight!"
- Do your best to avoid embarrassing your child in public or in front of her peers. This is often the time parents resort to social media shaming and other such tactics because they know that peer relationships matter. This is a major trust killer. If you must correct a child in front of her peers, do so discreetly so as to avoid social embarrassment.

Ages 13+

- To the best of your good judgment, be respectful of your teen's space and privacy. Unless you see a red flag, respecting his privacy conveys trust.
- Let your teen know that you value his opinions and feelings. The adolescent brain is growing and changing in miraculous ways. Emotions are higher during adolescence than during any other phase of life. What we may have perceived as drama before is likely authentically high emotional reactions.
- Get to know your child's brain so that you can better guide

him through this final stage of childhood. Check out Daniel Siegel's book *Brainstorm*, which is a terrific resource. Dr. Siegel also has several informative YouTube videos.

- Continue conveying your trust and belief in him. This is an ongoing process.

6

Defining Your Family Culture

> What greater thing is there for human souls than
> to feel that they are joined for life—to be with each
> other in silent unspeakable memories?
>
> —George Eliot

YOUR FAMILY CULTURE is the family experience you create. It
is a complex story of beliefs, attitudes, values, dispositions, expectations, habits, roles, and more. We typically think of only
countries or large societies as cultures, but sociologists say that
even individual families have their own cultures, and signifi-
cantly, research has found that family culture may play a more
important role in shaping a child than parent-
ing style.[11] Family cultures are powerful, creating the worlds in which children are raised,
and the type of culture a family creates
strongly predicts a child's happiness. **Happy
families intentionally create positive family cultures.** Parents
who do not intentionally create a family culture—who put little
to no thought into the values they want to instill and the family

*Happy families
intentionally create
positive family cultures.*

88

bonds they want to create, and who do not have a plan for building their family—will fall into a default culture that is created haphazardly as the years go by.

Seven Pillars of Family Culture

1. Values

Family values such as integrity, respect, honesty, responsibility for each other and the broader community, and fairness are taught by example. What you live, they will learn. It's counter-productive to say respect is a family value if disrespect is often shown in the home. These values should be upheld so that they become simply a way of being and relating. Your values are laid out in your mission statement (more on this later), so post it in a visible area and talk about them regularly. More important, live these values consistently.

2. Dispositions

The word *disposition* is defined in the *Oxford Dictionary* as "a person's inherent quality of mind and character," with the synonyms listed as *character*, *temperament*, and *mentality*. I think this also encompasses attitude and self-esteem. Let's break this down into bite-size pieces.

What is your character? Your partner's? What about the quality of your mind? Are you positive or negative—glass half-full or half-empty? What about your temperament? Are you generally calm and laid-back or are you wound a little tighter? Are you easily angered or can you let things roll off? Are you easy to get along with? Are you a perfectionist? Do you think highly of yourself, or do you have poor self-esteem?

All of these things play into the environment your children are growing up in, and they are a piece of the family culture puzzle. It's likely that you and your partner have different answers to these questions. My husband is more positive and laid-back. I'm more of a perfectionist and easily thrown off. Our children have picked up our different characteristics and traits. One child is more anxious, like me. The other is happy-go-lucky, like Dad. Did they inherit those traits or learn them? I have no idea—probably a bit of both. The point is that it's important to learn and respect each other and to find ways for all of the different dispositions in the home to live in harmony.

Did you know that self-esteem can be contagious? In an article titled "Is Low Self-Esteem Contagious?" Katie Hurley states, "Research published in the *Journal of Personality and Social Psychology* suggests that while positive re-framing from friends and loved ones can enhance self-esteem in people struggling with low self-esteem, consoling a friend with low self-esteem can be exhausting and can make those doing the consoling feel worse about themselves. This suggests that self-esteem can actually be contagious. The flip side, of course, is that positivity can also be contagious."[12] It is important, therefore, to take good care of yourself and do the self-work needed to become a positive person. It's much easier to be a positive parent when you're feeling positive!

3. Expectations

This is a fairly broad topic that extends beyond your expectations of your children and beyond the scope of this book, but I'll attempt to summarize it here.

Yes, what you expect of your children is very important, and I don't simply mean expecting him to clean his room. I'm talking about expecting him to be a good person, to be able to meet challenges with perseverance, and to have the ability to make wise decisions and learn from poor ones.

This also includes what you expect of your partner because it sets an example of what your children should expect from theirs one day. Moreover, it teaches them about gender roles, which will influence how they treat people of the opposite sex as well as how they treat same-sex peers.

Going beyond relationship expectations, children learn your expectations of society, of people of different cultures and races, of employers and jobs, of government and politicians and restaurant servers and firefighters. They learn what you expect regarding lack or abundance, bad luck or good, hardship or blessings. Your expectations are often passed right on to your children and suddenly you have a whole house of expectations, and those expectations play a vital role in your family culture.

4. Habits

Just like everything else, our children pick up our habits—the good ones, the bad ones. Does someone have a habit of yelling? It isn't hard to see how that affects the family culture. The habit of eating dinner together several times a week affects it, too.

Try to form and/or continue positive habits; a good rule of thumb is if you don't want your children to pick it up, it's best to drop it. This really only applies to habits, because as a general rule, children will pick up most things you drop, including Cheetos and possibly bits of cat food, and they often eat what they pick up. Just a fair warning.

5. Communication

We've gone over communication quite a lot in this book because it is so crucial to building strong family bonds, and so it makes sense that it's also crucial to your family culture. Which family is happier—the one who uses positive, respectful communication or the one who blames, criticizes, and yells? Of course, positive communication builds positive bonds, so work on those communication skills.

6. Conflict resolution

This is an aspect of communication, but it is so important in building a positive family culture that it deserves its own discussion. It is absolutely vital to model peaceful conflict resolution, to teach it to your child, and to expect it from everyone in the home. When you put several different personalities under one roof, there is going to be conflict, and what you do with it can seriously make or break a relationship.

Steps to peaceful conflict resolution:

- Teach children to identify and manage emotions.
- Use time-in to bring the young child into a safe, calming

space and learn ways to calm down before talking through to a solution. Time-in is discussed in chapter 9.

- Older kids can use a peace table (see chapter 9) or peace circle, which takes the place of time-in around age seven.
- Teach positive communication (such as "I" statements) and not to place blame.

7. Traditions

Rituals and traditions solidify the family unit and help children to feel like they are part of something bigger than themselves. Daily routines were discussed in the previous chapter and play a big role in your family culture. Weekly traditions such as family movie night or pizza night, attending a spiritual service, or family meetings breathe life into your family blueprint. Traditions surrounding birthdays, holidays, reunions, and celebrations all place a building block in your intentional positive family culture.

Creating Your Family Blueprint

If you were going to build a house, you wouldn't just grab random materials and start throwing them together. You'd need a blueprint. The same is true when you're building a family culture. Drawing up a blueprint, or mission statement, will help you define your goals and serve as a reminder of your vision going forward. To intentionally build the family your heart desires, you need to know precisely what materials you'll need and how you'll put them together.

Your family blueprint outlines your goals, devises a plan to meet those goals, and puts that plan into action with step-by-step achievements to work toward. While you and your partner are spearheading the creation of this mission statement, every member of the family should take part in drafting it. By doing so, everyone feels invested in it. Uniting behind a shared set of goals will strengthen your family's connection.

The Benefits of a Blueprint

A good mission statement will define and motivate your family members. As mentioned previously, it will unite the family in a shared set of goals. Drafting a blueprint gives everyone in the family a voice and builds solidarity. Decision making will be easier because you know what doesn't serve your family's purpose. As you draft your blueprint, each family member will begin to evaluate his or her values, beliefs, desires, goals, and vision. Finally, the blueprint will become a "code of conduct" that you can refer to as a teaching tool with your children.

Your Legacy Begins Here

I've been giving a lot of thought lately to what my legacy will be. How will my children speak of me to their children and grandchildren? What will I be remembered for? Likewise, how do people of the community view our family? What contributions have we made? I hope to be remembered as a woman who gave love freely and without condition and who made a positive impact on those around her. I hope my family legacy is one of gentle kindness and integrity. What do you hope for your legacy?

Your family blueprint will eventually become your family legacy. Draft it with great care. If you are intentional about the goals you write down and about seeing them through to fruition, you will leave a legacy to be proud of. The truth is that we all leave our marks on this world. We all leave some kind of legacy; not everyone leaves a good one. I know you desire to leave a positive personal and family legacy that

Your family blueprint will eventually become your family legacy. Draft it with great care.

will whisper your good name for generations to come. Your family blueprint will guide you every step of the way.

Drafting Your Blueprint

Your blueprint will come to be through a family discussion of your values, beliefs, morals, dreams, and goals. In order for this blueprint to be successful, each family member must engage in the conversation. It's important that everyone is heard and respected as they give their ideas. Write each person's answers down as you go. Even very young children should be present during this discussion. This is where they begin to learn and understand the importance of the family unit.

It's useful to start with a list of values. For example, our family values include time, learning, togetherness, gentleness, slowness, and presence. Jot down all the values your family members list. You can pare them down to what is most important and agreeable for everyone at a later time, once a good, hardy list has been compiled.

Next, list your beliefs. Whether or not you are religious, you undoubtedly have deep-seated beliefs about the meaning of life, how people should be treated, and so on. For example, my family believes that all humans deserve to be treated with respect and kindness. We believe in caring for orphans and children in poverty. We believe in helping animals in need and caring lovingly for pets.

Finally, list your goals, individually and as a family. From cultivating more self-control to making the team to raising emotionally intelligent children or starting your own business—whatever you envision for yourself and for your family, write it down, along with everyone else's visions.

Once you have a comprehensive list of values, beliefs, and goals, have another meeting (or several) to really nail down the mission of your family. Write out the final product, have each family member sign it, and place it somewhere highly visible. Refer to it as often as necessary, and at least once a month.

As your family grows and your children age, it's a good idea to review and reevaluate your mission yearly. This is a way of renewing the vision and keeping everyone on the same page.

Now that you know *what* you want to build, it's time to figure out *how* to build it. This is where you'll expand on your blueprint like a flow chart. Take each value and write how to live that value. For example, your entries may look like this:

Slowness: We will not take on too many extracurricular activities and will ensure we have plenty of downtime together.

Gentleness: We will not tolerate harsh words or actions. If one family member treats another family member in a non-gentle manner, it will be that person's responsibility to repair the relationship and do a kind deed.

Do the same for your beliefs. How will you live in accordance with your beliefs?

We believe in caring for the earth. We will recycle, conserve energy and water, and pick up trash in our community once a month.

We believe all animals deserve kindness. Once every three months, we will volunteer at the animal shelter. During winter, we will take blankets and other needed items to the shelter. We will care for our own pets lovingly.

Finally, do this same thing for your goals.

I want to make the baseball team. I will practice every day and ask for advice from the coach.

I want to have a strong relationship with my children when they are adults. I will show them respect and unconditional love while they grow and will have faith that they will show it back to me when they're grown.

I want to have a vibrant marriage. I will commit to effective communication and showing my love every day. I will enrich our relationship through focused time together.

Here are some questions to get you started in making your own family blueprint.

1. What kind of family do we want to be?
2. What values will we uphold?
3. What kind of atmosphere do we want in our home?
4. What kind of relationships do we want to have with one another?
5. Who inspires us and why?

The Value of Routines and Rituals

Your family culture may be drafted at the table, but it is built in day-to-day life. Routines and rituals are vital ingredients for the culture you're creating. Children thrive with regular, consistent, and predictable routines. Routines allow children to feel safe and provide emotional stability as they learn that they can trust the adults to provide what they need. This frees them to do their "work" of playing and exploring. Routines should be comfortable and flexible—more like a daily flow than a rigid by-the-clock schedule. As children learn their daily flow, they begin to understand what is important to the family and where they fit in. It teaches responsibility and how to constructively manage themselves and their space.

Maintaining consistent daily routines can help children to deal with stressful events when they arise, such as the birth of a sibling or a move to a new city. Additional benefits of routines include teaching younger children good hygiene habits such as brushing teeth and handwashing, developing basic work skills and time management, and setting body clocks. Children who have a predictable bedtime routine tend to get sleepy at the same time nightly and fall asleep more easily than children without regular routines.

By adding choices to your child's daily routine, you can empower him and give him more of a sense of control over his daily rhythm. **Power struggles often occur because children feel they have little to no control over their daily lives.** Giving a child some control over his routine and rhythm reduces these power struggles.

Routines are helpful for parents as well because they generally make the day run more smoothly. Knowing what to expect elicits better behavior from your children and results in less stress for the family. Routines allow you to be more efficient in completing your daily tasks and allows you to give fewer instructions as children become accustomed to the routine.

Power struggles often occur because children feel they have little to no control over their daily lives.

Your family is unlike any other, and the routines you set will be as unique as you are. If you find that a routine isn't working, be flexible and work with your family to establish one that is effective. The following are some ideas for routines throughout the stages of childhood.

Infants

Infants do not need a set routine. We should feed them when they are hungry and let them nap when they are sleepy. Over time, they naturally develop a routine of sorts, and all we need to do is facilitate this, such as making their rooms comfortable and conducive to sleep and feeding them in a predictable and soothing way. Eventually, you can use your infant's natural schedule to build a routine that works for her and the whole family.

Toddlers and Preschoolers

Toddlers and preschoolers especially thrive on routines. This is a good time to create a visual chart or poster to help guide them through the rhythm of their day. Use both photos and written words placed in the order to be completed, and refer to this chart often throughout the day. Your daily flow may go something like this:

- get dressed
- brush teeth
- breakfast
- playtime
- crafts

- cleanup
- lunch
- music
- free play
- dinner

- cleanup
- bath
- story
- bedtime

Building small rituals into your routines will make it fun for your child. Singing a song during dressing in the morning or special rituals at bath time will add joy and connection to your day. Giving your toddler advance notice of transition is respectful and helpful in reducing meltdowns. "We will leave the park in ten minutes." "We have five minutes left, and then we are leaving." "Okay, time to go. Let's race to the car!"

Another example of using routine to transition is when dropping your child off at school or childcare. Perhaps every day, you sing the same song on the way to the establishment, skip to the front door together, give a hug and kiss, say the same little rhyme or catchphrase (such as "See you later, alligator"), and wave good-bye with a smile. This predictable little ritual leaves your child with positive feelings to start his day.

School-Age Children

School-age children can take more responsibility for themselves and their environments. It may be helpful to establish routines around school mornings, homework, hobbies/sports, cleaning up, chores, and bedtime. Setting routines around these particular daily events will reduce stress. For example, having a designated place for homework and a set time to begin it each day is likely to cut down on arguments over getting it done, especially if you are consistent, kind, and matter-of-fact. Some children like having charts to tick off. Setting these routines with your child's input will increase cooperation.

Adolescents

Adolescents should be able to manage their routines with little supervision from you. They may still need your help and guidance, but in general, they should be well adjusted to the family routines by now.

Rituals

Earlier I mentioned building in small rituals such as singing during dressing in the morning or on the way to school drop-off. Rituals become the warm memories your child will look back on and cherish for a lifetime. Becky Bailey, PhD, says, "The goal of rituals is connection. Rituals create sacred space designated for togetherness and unity." Anything that you do together repeatedly, such as a walk after dinner or Sunday waffles, becomes a ritual. Chances are you have already created several rituals, and those are providing several benefits to your child. Dr. Steven Wolin, a psychiatrist at the George Washington University, says, "If you grow up in a family with strong rituals, you're more likely to be resilient as an adult."[13] Researchers have also found that children who have family rituals fare better emotionally in times of distress. At the very least, you know you're creating shared identity and a sense of structure and belonging.

Here are some ideas to spur your creativity in creating your family rituals.

- Every year on his birthday, my husband woke up to a family member smearing butter on his nose. As odd as it is, it's a cherished memory for him. We haven't carried on the butter tradition, but we have created birthday rituals that include lots of balloons and crepe paper–covered doorways to run through. How can you make the day special for your loved one?
- When Halloween draws near, I blow up several white balloons and draw ghost faces on them. I hang them around

outside our home, and just as it gets dark, we get our ghost-hunting gear and pop some ghosts.

- The Christmas season is filled with rituals, such as gathering old toys to donate and the always disastrous-looking gingerbread house.
- I grew up on a steady diet of Scrabble and Boggle. Family game night is a great idea but not so easy to fit into our busy lives. Schedule it in and turn off everything that dings, rings, or buzzes, unless it's part of the game!
- Bedtime storybooks are great, but my boys crave a made-up animated adventure. The space projection from their nightlight has inspired many memorable travels as we've found treasures, defeated dragons and aliens, and discovered new planets!
- Our New Year's Eve countdown consists of balloons with written activities inside that we pop each hour, an annual *Minute to Win It*–style tournament, and too much confetti.
- It's a good idea to build rituals around transition times of the year, such as back-to-school and seasonal rituals. Plant seeds in the spring. Go camping in the summer. Visit a pumpkin patch in the fall. Go sledding in the winter.
- Unplug for a set amount of time each evening. No phones or tablets allowed! Being able to depend on this quality time together every day will do wonders for your children and family.

A Culture of Peace—Taming Sibling Rivalry

When I gave birth to my second child, I was, for the first time in my life, tossed rather abruptly into the complexities of a sibling relationship. As an only child, I'd had fanciful ideas of living in harmony with a best friend for life. Perhaps like I did, you imagined your children would be best friends, playing together, giggling with each other, walking hand in hand . . . But then reality struck, and you found yourself being the referee in continual sibling battles. You don't have to tolerate sibling rivalry in the name of "normal." Sure, it *is* normal for children who live under the same roof to occasionally have a disagreement, but cultivating strong sibling bonds is important for maintaining peace in the home and creating a positive family culture. It is important to intentionally focus on minimizing sibling rivalry, teach your children how to navigate their relationship in a positive and respectful manner, and provide an environment that allows their relationship to flourish.

When it comes to sibling rivalry, parents often unwittingly spark the fires we've spent days and even years trying to extinguish. I've certainly made my share of mistakes in fueling rivalry. I've also since learned how to create more peace. In this section, I'll share with you my mistakes and victories in creating a culture of peace between my children.

Mistake No. 1: Comparisons

I knew that comparing my children wasn't a bright idea, but it's hard not to let a comparison slip out sometimes. "Your brother was potty trained by now. Why are you making this difficult?" Guess how helpful that was in both teaching him to use the potty and creating warm and fuzzy feelings for his brother? If you answered not helpful at all, you're correct.

Comparisons can have two outcomes. One is resentment toward the "better" sibling, and the other is a feeling of inadequacy or low self-concept. Even when you're giving one the "favorable" comparison—for example, telling her she is so much more responsible than her sibling—this sets up a competitive atmosphere. Dr. Laura Markham, author of *Peaceful Parent, Happy Siblings*, says, "The problem is that comparisons reinforce the way we think about our children, and therefore shape the way we treat them. Maybe even worse, every comparison we make may encourage our children to compare themselves."[14] Instead of comparing, describe what you see, what you like, what needs to change, or what needs to be done, but leave the other children out of it. Instead of saying, "Why can't you do your homework without a fuss like your brother?" describe what needs to be done. "You have homework that needs to be completed before TV time."

Mistake No. 2: Labeling

Did you and your siblings get labeled when you were growing up? Was it openly accepted that one was "the smart one" or "the pretty one" or "the talented one"? It seems I have accidentally

labeled one of my boys "the funny one." I didn't do this by saying, "Hey, you're funny, and your brother isn't!" Apparently it
happened rather covertly simply because I laughed at him more
and said things like, "You are so funny!" His brother would almost always pipe up, "Am I funny, too?" Then he frequently
sought to "measure up" with performances meant to make us
laugh just as much.

This is a tricky situation, because how can a parent celebrate
the strengths and accomplishments of one child without fueling the competition? I think the key is to make sure that every
child feels loved enough, valued enough, and good about himself. The fix for us was not to stop laughing at my child's hilari-
ousness, but to find something about his brother that we
brought to light equally and celebrated.

Victory No. 1: Acknowledge the Bond

I made a point to notice and point out when my boys were
kind to each other or playing well together. There is something
to be said for speaking out about what you want to have happen in your life. I've read this in many articles about positivity,
and it turns out that it works amazingly well. *What you focus
on, you get more of.* When I focused on their rivalry, I got more
of it. When I focused on their connection, things improved
greatly.

Victory No. 2: Create a Team Atmosphere

In my family, we're a team, and we tackle things as a team instead of competing for stars or check marks. Rather than indi-

vidual chore charts, we have a team chart. Weekly family meetings are beneficial in creating a team atmosphere. In our meetings, we all have equal opportunity to weigh in on any issues we are facing and vacation planning, etc. By getting siblings involved in celebrating each other, such as by helping to decorate for a brother's or sister's birthday party or going to watch a sibling's performance, the message is, "We are all in this together." Family traditions and routines also foster a team/family atmosphere.

Victory No. 3: Set Clear Limits

Children deserve to feel safe and comfortable in their own homes, and unchecked sibling rivalry can make a home feel like anything but a safe haven. I don't expect my kids to always get along, or even to always like each other, but I do expect them to avoid resorting to violence, taunting, or name-calling. I expect them to remain respectful through their disagreements. This is a boundary that I have made clear to them. Set appropriate boundaries that respect each individual in the home and that create an atmosphere of acceptance and love, not rivalry and conflict.

When siblings argue, it is going to be your judgment call as to whether to step in. You won't always need to jump to the rescue. Give them some time to work it out, but step in if it escalates to violence, either physical or verbal. All children need to be taught basic conflict-resolution skills. Teach them to speak respectfully, to use "I" statements, and to take a break when things get heated, just as you learned to do in chapter 4. Realize, however, that these are skills that take time and age to develop. These are upstairs brain functions, so young children simply aren't always capable of this kind of logic and reasoning. It's still good to talk about it and practice it, but don't expect them to master it until much later. Keep teaching and holding your limits, and don't get discouraged. (I discuss limit setting and enforcing in chapter 9.) Many adults still struggle with communication and peaceful conflict resolution, which is all the more reason to start teaching your children early. What a difference we parents can make for the future!

Discussion Questions

1. What is your temperament? What is your partner's? Your child's? How can you promote respect and tolerance?

2. Are your expectations, habits, and attitudes in line with your values?

3. What does your family do regularly that could run more easily and smoothly with the introduction of a routine?

4. What, if anything, is preventing you from establishing a consistent routine?

5. List at least five rituals that you want to be a part of your family culture.

6. Do you occasionally compare your children to each other? Talk about how you can intentionally keep from making comparisons that fuel rivalry.

7. It's important to look for and acknowledge positive sibling interaction. Do you do this already? Will you

make it a point to do it daily and note any changes for at least one week?

Putting It into Practice

The foundation of the family life you want is built upon the vision you and your partner have, and the trust and connection you foster with each other and your children. When you create your blueprint, you put your vision on paper for the family to see. Because everyone takes part in designing it, your blueprint becomes the vision for your whole family, giving everyone direction and goals. Discuss your blueprint often. Family meetings are a good time to review it. If you create it and put it in a drawer, it won't serve its purpose. It must be discussed and lived every day, frequently brought to the spotlight in family meetings and when you correct your child for behaving out of line with what has been set forth. Keeping your blueprint in a prominent place in the home and discussing it often will help mold your family and bring your dreams to fruition.

1. Keep your blueprint in a prominent place in the home, visible to everyone.
2. Review your blueprint at family meetings, at least once a month.
3. Bring your blueprint into focus during correction. For example, "Our family mission statement says that we treat each other with kindness. It isn't kind to tell your brother he's stupid. That's not how we agreed to treat one another."

Take the five rituals you listed in discussion question 5 and create a plan to get started right away. For example, if you want to create a tradition of family game night, go ahead and plan one for the upcoming weekend. Buy a board game or search games on the Internet that you think your family would enjoy. Your attitude about the new tradition will rub off, so bring your excitement and positivity to the table when you announce the plan to your family.

If rivalry is a problem in your home, I recommend *Siblings Without Rivalry*, by Adele Faber and Elaine Mazlish, and the aforementioned *Peaceful Parent, Happy Siblings*, by Dr. Laura Markham. Here are some steps to begin a turnaround toward peace.

1. Pay attention to your words and actions to make sure you aren't unwittingly creating any rivalry.
2. Find something about each child to celebrate.
3. Set clear limits about violence, both physical and emotional. While disagreements happen, there is never a good reason for name-calling, aggression, or bullying of any kind, so be clear that those things will not be tolerated in the home. Refer to chapter 9 for ideas on limit enforcement without punishment.

It's not just the big life moments that define your family and shape your children, but it's also the ordinary, everyday moments. It's the environment they live in, the family traditions, the relationships they share, and the daily routines that make up childhood. How lucky our children are to have parents who lovingly and purposefully create positive family cultures, healthy relationships, and happy days. We are crafting beautiful childhoods. There isn't much glamour in showing up every single day for bedtime stories, kissing scrapes, wiping noses, and rocking babes, but there is no work more important than the work of parents, because you are helping to build a better future for the human race.

One tool I use to help focus on my goals is to write three daily intentions to start my day with. I keep this in the front of a binder, and I keep my binder on the kitchen table, where I pass by many times a day. Keep your intentions short, simple, meaningful, and totally doable. Think about your day ahead and what you need to address to bring a sense of calm and peace to your home. Here are some examples to get you started.

- I will spend at least 30 minutes in child-directed play without distractions.
- I will take 3 deep breaths before I respond to an agitating circumstance.
- I will tell my husband how much I appreciate him today.
- I will spend a little extra one-on-one time with my child today.
- I will not sign in to social media until my children are in bed.
- I will not sit on the bench at the park. I will play with my kids.
- I will do something romantic for my spouse this evening.
- I will feed myself nutritious food today, not leftovers from the kids' plates.
- I will exercise for at least 30 minutes today.

- I will not allow negative thoughts to take residence in my mind.
- I will choose love today.
- I will treat myself to a warm bath and light music tonight.
- I choose to be happy today.

7

Seeing Children in a New Way

A person's a person, no matter how small.
—Dr. Seuss

I WAS EMOTIONAL. I was feeling sad and overwhelmed and had been for days. Finally, I couldn't fight back the tears any longer. My two boys were busy playing superheroes, and so I went into my bedroom, sank down on the far side of the bed, where I thought I'd be hidden from sight in case my superheroes' adventure led them past my door, and I began to sob. The tears flowed until my eyes were puffy and my nose was red. My six-year-old came into the room and looked at my face. He removed his mask, laid his sword down on the bed, and without saying a word, he sat next to me and just put his arms around me. He held me for several minutes, his kind eyes and gentle embrace saying all that needed to be said at that moment. This is the true heart of a child.

I didn't always see his beautiful heart. Just three years prior,

I had a very different story. I was so focused on his misbehavior that I was missing the compassion he has for all people and animals and the light that shines from his sensitive soul. I spent my days correcting him, putting him in time-out over and over. I believed every infraction had to be dealt with or he would believe he could get away with poor behavior. I had been warned that was true. So, our days were filled with tears and struggle, and I greatly missed the loving bond I'd shared with him when he was an infant. I longed just to hold him in my lap, to rock him again, to stroke his hair while his little arms were wrapped around me. Yet, there we were, battling for control, more disconnected than ever before. My heart broke, and I began searching for answers—answers that led me to positive parenting.

I've been parenting this way for six years now, not perfectly but consistently. Still, when my sons display childlike behavior in public, when their laughter gets too loud and I feel the stares of the strangers around me, I can feel my cheeks flush and the urge to silence them quickly. Then, I remind myself that it's okay for children to be childlike, and that maybe, just maybe, if we all were a little more childlike—if we laughed a little louder, if we played a little harder, if we noticed with wonder the wind on our faces and took time to remark on how nice it feels, if we could slow down our fast-paced adult lives and see through the eyes of a child again—perhaps then we'd all have more joy.

Children do not enter this world with bad intentions

I've realized that **children do not enter this world with bad intentions**. They do not come to wear us out, test our patience, or push us over the edge. They come to us with a need for love, connection, and belonging. Yet, we've been taught to make them earn those things only through abiding by our rules and obeying our commands. We don't give these things freely. What if we did? What if we satisfied the needs of their human hearts and never threatened to jerk it away? Imagine a generation of satisfied hearts!

Imagine a world where we choose to see children in a different light. What if we always looked at them with the same awe and wonder as we did when they were first put in our arms? What if we didn't allow negative warnings about "the terrible twos" and other fearmongering messages to get into our heads and skew our perceptions?

Can we see our children's motives as pure and not conniving? Can we view our kids as blessings, here to love and learn? We can if we choose to perceive them that way. How we perceive our children determines how we relate to them.

Unfortunately, the way children are viewed in our culture has caused us to relate to them poorly. We perceive attention seeking where there is only a desire to connect, clinginess where there is only a motive for love, disobedience where there is only a will to learn, and defiance where there is only a need to grow. We view them as manipulative, conniving, and selfish, and we base our interactions with them on those views.

We have a tendency to reduce children to nothing more than their behavior.

Children are more than their ability to sleep through the night. They are more than their willingness to instantly obey. They are more than a grade. They are more than a mood. They are more than the behavior they display at any given moment, more than what we see on the surface. They are human beings—messy and beautiful, wild and compassionate, and worth getting to know, not just getting to mind.

Let's look a little deeper today at what it means to be a child, not just what it takes to raise one.

Society expects children to act like mature little adults, and this unreasonable expectation puts undue pressure on parents to have their children perform well, especially in public. Children are not small adults. Their brains have a lot of developing to do. Often, we punish them for something they have absolutely no control over: an underdeveloped brain. We assume they have negative intentions toward us when in reality they do not.

Let's look a little deeper today at what it means to be a child, not just what it takes to raise one.

With expectations that children should act like adults comes great disappointment when they act like children. Many parents find solace, it seems, in discussing their disappointments with other parents, sometimes even in the presence of their children. Parents say this makes them feel better, as though they are not alone. I wonder, though, do they stop to think how it makes the child feel?

I overheard the following statements recently, all said in the presence of children:

"I can't wait for school to start back," one mom said. "He has driven me crazy all summer!" Her son stood beside her, looking down at the floor.

"Is yours a good baby? Gosh, mine's not! He's a whiny baby," said the mother of a toddler in the pediatrician's waiting room.

"Mine are spoiled brats," a woman told the lady in the checkout line. Her children were sitting in the cart, hearing the message loud and clear.

None of these children said a word. None of them spoke up and said, "Wow, Mom. That really hurts my feelings."

Just because children aren't quite articulate enough to verbally express their feelings of deep shame and hurt doesn't mean they aren't feeling it.

Why do we find it acceptable to speak so terribly to and about our children in their presence? Do we think they don't understand? How can we believe they won't understand cutting words such as "mine are spoiled brats" yet expect them to understand more complex ideas such as social propriety? Or do we think that our harsh words will somehow motivate them? Again, it's cultural conditioning at play. Sadly, it is culturally acceptable to treat children in this manner. It seems almost expected, actually, to complain about how annoying our kids are and how much we have to sacrifice for them. It seems this is one way we increase parent-to-parent bonding. Yet, I oppose this idea that belittling them in their presence will somehow motivate them to be better children. If shaming ever works as a motivator, it is with a high price.

Dr. Brené Brown has spent the past twelve years researching shame, guilt, and vulnerability. In her book *The Gifts of Imperfection*,[15] she says, "Shame, blame, disrespect, betrayal, and the withholding of affection damage the roots from which love grows." Those cutting words? They're damaging. And she very poignantly notes, "Shame corrodes the very part of us that believes we are capable of change."[16]

That's big. That deserves our attention.

Children, like all human beings, feel most cooperative when they are treated with respect and kindness. Adults do not respond well to people who speak to us harshly or treat us with disrespect. Is it a stretch to believe that children wouldn't respond well to such treatment either? Think of how it might feel if a loved one spoke so unkindly of you in front of your peers, or threatened you when you were feeling your worst. I doubt you would feel motivated in any way, yet we seldom stop to think of how this treatment makes children feel. We are habituated to seeing children as inferior rather than inexperienced, when in truth, that's what they really are—inexperienced humans doing the best they can with what they've been given up to this point. How can we expect anything more?

If we want to create lasting bonds with our children, we need to change the way we see them. We need a huge cultural shift in the way we view children, and it starts with you and me. We can assume they have good intentions, not bad. We can perceive the behavior as communication, not manipulation.

Tune out the clamor of society and tune in to the whispers of your heart. These are not tyrants. They are not our enemies. These are our precious children.

We don't have to surrender our inner voices. **Tune out the clamor of society and tune in to the whispers of your heart. These are not tyrants. They are not our enemies. These are our precious children.**

Here's a liberating truth that I've discovered: It's okay to be tender. Love isn't really supposed to be tough. Being tender doesn't open the door for a child to walk all over you. Being tender opens the door that allows your child to walk alongside you. When she's walking alongside you, she hears the words you say. When you're walking alongside her, you can guide her steps. Tenderness is the avenue to connection, and connection is the key to parenting. And it all starts with choosing to see our children in a new way.

If we are going to see children in a new way, then we must also see parenthood in a new way. Rather than being the strict authoritarian (which is a role we take on when we perceive the child is out to do bad things), we can take on the much more connecting role of teacher and guide. Instead of chastising him harshly (a duty we perceive necessary to make the child good), we can be an encourager (because we understand he is already good).

Think about this. The people in our lives who look past our faults and see our beauty, the ones who still see the light in us during the times we feel only darkness, those are the people who save us from the depths of blackness. Those are the ones who help us see our own beauty and light again. Do you have someone in your life like that? We all need that person—the one who sees our light. The one who reflects our light back at us so we can see it, too. That's what a parent should be.

You may be wondering how this is going for me. How are my kids doing? Well, I won't say that they are perfect. I won't say I am either. But I will say that they are beautiful people. My older son took his birthday money and bought his brother a gift. He said, "I have enough, and I just want my brother to be happy." He sponsors a needy child through Compassion International and works every month to pay the sponsor fee. He tells me he wishes he could sponsor them all. This past Christmas, upon seeing that I had filled their stockings but mine was empty, my two gently parented boys took it upon themselves to secretly stuff my stocking with handwritten love notes and left-over Halloween candy. That's hardly the behavior of "spoiled, disrespectful brats."

You see, some parents may measure success with grades or compliments of good behavior from onlookers or tidy rooms and completed chore charts, but I measure success with kindness and compassion. So far, I'd say positive parenting has definitely been a success. Although my sons do get good grades and are "well behaved," what matters is that they have empathy and compassion, because that's what I want to send out into this world. That's what the world needs more of.

Our home is a safe haven. Even though my children argue sometimes, they forgive quickly and move on. They are the best of friends, and I have no doubt that they will have each other's backs always. They trust us. We trust them. We are close, and everyone knows they're loved. I can't really ask for more than that.

Discussion Questions

1. How do you perceive children ? How does that perception affect how you treat them?

2. Do you feel the pressure for your children to behave like adults, especially in public? Does their childish behavior embarrass you? Is it their behavior or your expectations that is really the problem?

3. How do you speak about your children to others in front of them? Are your words uplifting or crushing? Before you speak, it can be useful to run your words through this filter: *How would I feel if someone said this about me?*

Putting It into Practice

Changing the way I saw my older son and his behavior was the first major step in my shift to positive parenting. Will you vow to be the one person in your child's life who always sees her light and reflects it back to her? That starts by looking for positive motives, even when she does something "bad."

When you see your child's motives as negative, you'll get triggered. You may become angry, embarrassed, or frustrated, and you may worry that she will grow up to be a bad person if you don't change her now. In this triggered state, you can justify making the child feel bad, because you're doing it to make her better in the long run. So, now you scold her, highlighting her character flaws and making her feel bad about herself. Unfortunately, because you're reflecting back the negative things that you see in her, she may *We behave how we see ourselves* incorporate this negative view into her self-concept, and see herself as a bad person. **We behave how we see ourselves,** so this can become a vicious cycle.

If you choose to see positive intent, however, you understand that your child isn't a bad person but rather just needs guidance about this issue. Even though you still correct her behavior, your tone and attitude are entirely different just because of how you view her intent. Feeling like she is a good person with positive motives who made a poor choice allows you to bring compassion to your correction, and that allows her to take it in without damaging her developing self-concept.

Let's look through two different lenses at the same scenario.

Mason comes running to tell you that his sister, Mia, spilled red juice. Mia says she did not! Her lips are red: You know she's been drinking red juice.

Negative intent: She's a sneaky little liar! "You liar! I see the juice stains on your mouth! Mason was honest. Why wouldn't you just be honest with me? I'm very disappointed in you. It's wrong to lie."

"Liar" is not a label you want to stick. If a child thinks she's a liar, she'll be a liar. Then if she gets punished for being a liar, she'll become a sneaky liar. Self-fulfilling prophecy! You just created what you feared.

Positive intent: She doesn't want to get in trouble or disappoint me. "Hmm. I see cherry red lips. I value your honesty. Were you drinking juice and it accidentally spilled? Sometimes I spill things by accident. No big deal. We just need to clean it up. Come help me."

Doesn't the tone feel much different in those scenarios? The first one probably leaves Mia feeling like a terrible person. She may feel a bit of guilt in the second one for spilling the juice, but she certainly doesn't get shamed or berated. She cleans up her mess, and all is forgiven.

Let's turn our attention to Mason for a moment. He's just "turned in" his sister for spilling the juice. Here is an opportunity to foster rivalry and reinforce tattling, which is exactly what happens in scenario one. He gets the praise for being honest. Now he might look for more opportunities to turn in his sister. She's not only feeling bad about herself, but I'd bet she's feeling resentful toward her brother, too. In scenario two, Mason simply witnesses a problem being solved. Because he sees that problems are something to be solved, not punished, he learns no value in tattling. Furthermore, no sibling rivalry is fueled because Mason is left out of the conversation you have with Mia.

Your assignment: Look for the positive motives behind your child's behavior. If you believe and convey that you believe she's a good person, she'll believe she is, too.

8

Raising Emotionally Healthy Children

One generation full of deeply loving parents would change the brain of the next generation, and with that, the world. —Dr. Charles Raison

As I MENTIONED in chapter 4, many of us have learned to offer only conditional love. We have been led to believe that unconditional love is "soft" and spoils kids, so many of our conventional parenting practices revolve around this idea that we should not be too tender with children. There are all sorts of frightening theories as to what may happen if we are "too easy" on them. It's difficult for parents to tune out all of this noise and listen to intuition instead.

Again, I wish to emphasize that positive parenting does not mean coddling children, tiptoeing around their feelings in an effort to ensure they are never upset, or failing to set boundaries. The goal is emotionally healthy children, and unconditional love is crucial to emotional health and positive self-worth.

Psychologist Carl Rogers understood the need for unconditional love, or what he called *unconditional positive regard*. He believed that childhood experiences are one of the two primary sources that influence a person's self-concept, the other one being evaluation by others. According to Rogers, we want to feel and behave in ways that are consistent with our self-image. He viewed the child as having two basic needs: positive regard from other people and self-worth.

A child with high self-worth, in Rogers's view, faces challenges well, accepts failure and unhappiness at times, and is open with people, whereas the child with low self-worth avoids challenges, cannot accept that life will be painful sometimes, and is defensive and guarded with people. Rogers believed that self-worth is first formed from the interactions the child has with his or her mother and father.

He also believed that we need to be positively regarded by others. We need to feel valued and respected, be shown affection, and feel loved. He made the distinction between unconditional and conditional positive regard. Unconditional positive regard is unconditional love, in which the parents fully accept the child for who she is and positive regard is not withdrawn if the child does something wrong or makes a mistake.

In conditional positive regard, the child receives approval only when she is performing to the parents' expectations of behavior. Approval is withdrawn when she makes a mistake. Therefore, the child is not loved for who she is but on the condition that she behave in a way that makes the parents happy.[17]

Because unconditional love and emotional health go hand in

hand, I believe it is time to turn our backs on conventional practices that require us to withdraw love, affection, and acceptance, and step boldly into unconditional parenting. I call this courageous love because it does take courage to go against the grain. It takes courage to take a leap of faith. It takes courage to break old patterns. The world needs courageous parents raising emotionally healthy children.

It is time to rise up against the methods that clearly do emotional harm to our children.

It is time to rise up against the methods that clearly do emotional harm to our children. Unfortunately, the latest trends seem to be moving in the opposite direction. Shaming and humiliating children in the name of discipline is touted as good parenting. We talk tough against bullying in schools or on the Internet but practice it in our own homes. We recognize the great emotional harm and link to suicide caused by shame, humiliation, and bullying when it's caused by anyone other than a parent, yet for a parent, it is still simply child training, and for some reason that makes it okay.

It's not okay. If we are committed to raising emotionally healthy people, we need to let go of the fear that unconditional love will make them bad people. To do that, it's important to understand what it means to love without conditions, because I think too often we confuse it with loving without boundaries. Perhaps it has been thought that loving unconditionally means that any and all behavior is granted a hug and not corrected. This is a falsified view fueled by the fearmongering that keeps us holding tough love in high regard.

It is possible, and even necessary, for unconditional love and correction to coexist. Showing a child that your boundaries are fixed, consistent, and unshakable proves your ability as a leader and builds respect. Showing that your love is also fixed, consistent, and unshakable builds a child's self-worth.

It is possible, and even necessary, for unconditional love and correction to coexist.

In addition to showing your child unconditional love, there are many ways you can build his self-worth. These include:

- showing physical affection
- using positive body language, such as leaning in close to listen, looking him in the eyes when he speaks, smiling, nodding approval, and giving thumbs-up and high fives
- using words of encouragement and affirmation, and speaking kindly about him to others
- giving your undivided attention each day to connect and when he speaks, and acknowledging him warmly when he enters a room
- creating a positive environment where he is free to be who he is
- instilling a sense of belonging by creating tight family bonds and traditions, as well as being involved in the community and in groups outside the immediate family, such as Scouts, 4-H, sports, etc.
- making sure your expectations are in line with his abilities and stage of development
- creating an atmosphere that allows him to express his

opinions and show his feelings and lets him know he will be heard and respected

■ giving age-appropriate responsibilities and independence

If your child shows signs of low self-worth, begin building it daily by providing unconditional love as well as utilizing the other ideas outlined in this chapter. Treat her mistakes as opportunities to learn and grow, emphasize her specific strengths, accept her for who she is, and communicate every day, "I love you, I see you, I believe in you, and you matter." Here are some warning signs of low self-worth to be on the lookout for.

■ avoids challenges
■ gives up easily
■ has nervous habits
■ is withdrawn from others
■ acts out often
■ is overly concerned with or sensitive to others' opinions
■ makes negative statements about self or others

Fostering good self-esteem is part of raising emotionally healthy children, yet it isn't the only factor. It is widely accepted that childhood experiences are crucial to emotional health. The same is true for secure attachment. Family experiences play a vital role as well. Positive family relationships and experiences promote good emotional health. Positive communication is also an important ingredient in well-adjusted families. Each of these topics have been addressed in this book, which means you are well on your way to raising an emotionally healthy child. Other factors that influence emotional health that we haven't covered are schooling, outside social interactions, and genetic makeup.

Conscious parents make conscious choices regarding their child's education. Research all your options and weigh the pros and cons carefully before making a decision. There are options besides the nearest public school. Whatever you choose, your child can thrive if you remain positive, supportive, and encouraging and keep the lines of communication open. Provide opportunities for him to be involved in activities such as sports, volunteering, clubs, art, and music, where he can have positive social interaction. Finally, teach your child emotional intelligence—the skills needed to identify and manage his own emotions and recognize and understand the emotions of others.

For a child to reach her fullest potential, she must have good emotional health. She must feel valued, respected, and loved without condition by her parents. We are builders of self-worth, and we should always be mindful of that fact. Leave behind the methods that harm your child's self-esteem and learn ways to parent that support emotional health. Together, we can raise a generation of children who know what it is like to be whole, if only we are courageous enough to try.

Discussion Questions

1. What fears do you have about loving unconditionally?

2 Assess whether your child currently has a positive or negative self-worth.

3. Discuss what you do now to either build up or tear down your child and ways you can improve in this area.

4. Talk with your partner about ways unconditional love and correction can coexist. Specifically, how can you correct your child in a way that says, "What you have done is wrong," rather than, "Who you are is wrong"?

Putting It into Practice

You have been putting this chapter into practice since you began reading this book. One of the many benefits of positive parenting is good emotional health. Your emotional health matters, too! Here are some tips for boosting your own emotional health.

- Grow your circle of friends. It's important to have a support group of positive and encouraging people.
- Find your passion. Gardening, scrapbooking, painting, collecting—what's yours?
- Meditate, pray, and/or practice yoga. These natural stress busters will improve your mood.
- Say no to overcommitment. There is only one of you! Don't try to do the work of ten people.
- Stop being self-critical. Treat yourself like you're striving to treat your child—with empathy, respect, and gentleness.
- Get involved in something that makes you feel good

about yourself. Volunteer at an animal shelter or gather canned goods for a food bank. Helping others boosts self-esteem.

- Be optimistic and express gratitude.
- I won't tell you to get enough sleep because you may throw this book across the room. You're a parent. I get it. Try to sleep a little bit.

Mirror, Mirror

A fun way to boost your child's emotional intelligence is to have him look in a mirror and ask him to make the faces he would make in the following situations.

1. You dropped your ice cream cone. (sad)
2. You're going on vacation. (excited)
3. Your friend can't come over. (disappointed)
4. You hear a frightening noise. (scared)
5. Someone snatched your toy away. (anger)
6. You're opening a gift. It's what you've been wanting! (surprised)
7. You can't tie your shoes. (frustrated)
8. You've been running for an hour. (tired)
9. Make up your own!

Act It Out

Ask your child to act out situations that make her feel this way:

Happy	Frustrated	Disappointed
Worried	Cheerful	Shy
Sad	Angry	Nervous
Excited	Proud	Tired
Scared	Embarrassed	Surprised

9

Trading Punishment for Solutions

Discipline is helping a child solve a problem. Punishment is making a child suffer for having a problem.
—L. R. Knost

ONCE WE UNDERSTAND that misbehavior is really just a signal for help—a way for children to tell us they're not feeling good inside—we are free to move away from punishment. By definition, to punish is to deliberately make someone suffer. The hope in punishment is that the pain of suffering is enough to cause a child to think twice before committing that particular act again.

We are accustomed to training children through pain. Harsh words. A slap on the hand. A smack across the behind. Physical pain. Emotional pain. Social pain. We are fooled into thinking it's good because it works. Of course it works—for a while, at least—because children have a biological need to connect with their parents, and it is frightening to them when that connection is threatened. We naturally try to avoid pain, so the child may comply out of fear of being hurt by his parents. The truth is that children don't learn optimally this way. With pain, fear, and the threat of disconnection from a primary attachment figure, the fight-or-flight response is triggered, thereby bypassing the thinking brain and actually inhibiting learning.

It's important to question not just the effectiveness of punishment but the beliefs that often underlie it, which is that children are basically bad and will do bad things without the threat of punishment hanging over them. Seeing children in this negative way skews our perception of their behavior and lessens our empathy for their experiences. Moreover, believing that children are innately bad gives us justification in our minds to do bad things to them in order to make them good, and this is a treacherous path to follow because it leads to disconnection and broken bonds.

Let me be clear once more that positive parenting is not a permissive approach. Indeed, choices have consequences in life, and this is an important lesson for children to learn. Sometimes part of the solution may be that the child needs to experience the consequences of her wrongdoing. The goal, however, is to not make punishment a first-line, cure-all method of dealing with every infraction.

Look for solutions rather than punishment.

Look for solutions rather than punishment. Children need to learn how to fix their mistakes, not just pay for them.

You must keep your eye on the big picture: raising capable, kind, emotionally healthy adults—not just temporarily compliant children. Parents desire temporary compliance because it solves the problem for the moment. However, if a child doesn't receive proper instruction, the problem will arise again and again. If you manage to make him too fearful through punishment to repeat the behavior, you still have only taught him what not to do. This leaves a rather wide gap in his education.

Here's another problem. When your knee-jerk reaction is to dish out punishment, you miss entirely what caused the misbehavior in the first place, you miss the chance to understand and connect with the child, you miss the chance to teach, and you rob the child of the responsibility of her actions. Once you've taken away a privilege or given a spanking or placed her in the time-out chair, you've essentially taken the responsibility of the child's actions upon yourself. You have deemed it your job to correct the problem by making her pay the consequence. Now, in the child's eyes, she has paid for her transgression, and that's the end of it. She has "done her time." Sure, she may have had to sit on the step and miss playtime, or she may have lost the privilege of going out with her friends, and these things are certainly aversive, but she's learned zero problem-solving skills. Give the responsibility back to the person it belongs to: the child. She needs to fix the problem. She needs to learn better skills. It's your responsibility to help her learn, not to fix everything for her. By holding children accountable for their actions, we raise responsible people.

How do you move from knee-jerk punishment to solution-oriented discipline?

First, look for the reason behind the behavior. Remember that behavior is communication—it is a clue to the internal state of a person. We act based on how we feel, so children who act bad likely are feeling bad on the inside. It could be something as simple as hunger or fatigue, or a deeper issue such as a problem with a friendship or feeling disconnected from a loved one. The first question to always ask yourself is "What is this behavior telling me?"

Second, remember to discipline yourself before you attempt to discipline your child. (Refer back to chapter 2.) An undisciplined parent cannot effectively discipline a child. Meeting an out-of-control child when you're an out-of-control parent results in a lot of chaos and hurt that only add to the problem. It is best to wait until you can approach the situation with a rational brain (that means you're not triggered and upset). It's okay to say, "I need a few minutes to myself, and then we'll talk about this."

Third, connect by conveying your understanding—and yes, your love—to your child. Connecting with a misbehaving child isn't a reward; it's a lifeline. He doesn't need to get his way all the time, but he always needs to get your love. Connecting has nothing to do with indulging, coddling, or spoiling children. Connection doesn't give in. Connection *understands*. Connection doesn't coddle. Connection *listens*. The boundary still stands, but so does your love, and that is reassuring to an out-of-control child.

Fourth, seek a solution to the problem. Your child should now be calm enough—through your connection—to release from fight-or-flight mode and think logically. Of course, this largely depends on the age and maturity of the child. A two-year-old can't come up with a solution on her own. So for her, it'd be something simple like, "I won't let you hit your sister. Come sit by me." A five-year-old can start offering ideas to fix the problem but still needs quite a bit of guidance. The following phrases are helpful to get the ball rolling: "How are you going to fix this?" "We have a problem. Can you think of a way to solve it?" She may need a nudge in the right direction, but let her do most of the brain work. Children over the age of eight can typically come up with a solution with little help, especially if they've had practice. Just make sure that whatever the solution is, it is followed through.

If your child refuses to come up with a solution and carry it out, then you'll have to flex your (kind and loving) parental muscle by telling him your solution and making sure he sees it through. You may also need to do that if this is not a new problem but a situation in which the child knows the rules and a better solution, but willfully made the wrong choice anyway. Connected children are still children, and they make poor decisions occasionally, too.

The final step is restoration and reconnection. Restoration is reestablishing trust and rebuilding the self-concept. During the restoration phase, the goal is to restore your child's feelings of self-worth. He should always come out the other side of discipline feeling like you believe he is a good person, regardless of his occasional slip-ups. Reconnection comes through leaving the incident in the past where it belongs and moving forward in good spirits.

Summary of Solution-Oriented Discipline

1. Look behind the behavior. Remember that behavior is communication, so figure out what the child's behavior is communicating about her internal state.
2. Discipline yourself first. Wait until you are calm and rational before you deal with the problem.
3. Connect with your child. The basic human needs of

love and connection must be met before the brain is free
to learn the lesson you want to teach.

4. Seek a solution. Teach your child to be a problem solver.
Teach her to right her wrongs and repair relationships.
This approach serves her much better than just "making
her pay."

5. Restore and reconnect. Make sure your child's self-
worth is restored and she understands that mistakes are
opportunities to learn and that a bad decision doesn't
mean she's a bad child. Reconnect through empathy
and love and moving forward in good spirits, leaving
the mistake in the past.

From Time-Out to Time-In

Toddlers and most preschoolers aren't developmentally ready to
problem solve. This is a function of the upstairs brain, which is
still very underdeveloped in young children. That means we
have two primary jobs when disciplining wee ones. The first is
to work on building and strengthening the neural connections
that will enable them to problem solve well in the future (we do
this through teaching them to calm themselves and through
repetitiously teaching the steps of problem solving). The second
is to act as their upstairs brain, making logical choices for them
until they are better able to do so.

Let's look at the conventional discipline method of time-
out. Time-out started being recommended in place of spanking
once we learned how harmful that practice was. Here's what
psychologist Gordon Neufeld says about time-out: "Unfortunately, we didn't realize what children needed and that the most

wounding experience of all is facing separation. If we knew that and understood it, we wouldn't be using it as punishment." The fear of separation may stop the behavior, and so we think we've won. However, the desire to be good afterward is coming from a place of insecurity, and that's the last place we want it to come from! What's more, when we punish a child through withdrawing affection and warmth and isolate him, we are appealing to his downstairs, reptilian brain, activating that primal response of fear. Drs. Siegel and Bryson, authors of *No-Drama Discipline*, call this "poking the lizard." It is much more beneficial to appeal to that developing upstairs brain. Finally, time-out often brings about feelings of anxiety and aggression in children. Sitting in a chair for several minutes may stop a behavior for all the wrong reasons, but it doesn't help a child to do better. **We can't expect children to do better until we give them the tools they need to succeed.**

> *We can't expect children to do better until we give them the tools they need to succeed.*

Time-in differs from time-out because the focus is on connection first and teaching second. Connection is what engages the upstairs brain. Remember, this is where logic and reasoning take place. While still very underdeveloped, it is growing, and through providing empathy and connecting with a child, we can aid her in growing a better brain. When we empathize and connect, we show a child that we get her, we understand the feelings and thoughts that motivated the behavior. This doesn't mean we accept the behavior. Connection calms the activity in the lower brain and helps the child to access her thinking brain, which she'll need to understand the lesson you want to teach. Children who are locked in fear cannot learn. Once connection is made and the upstairs brain is engaged, then you teach the child how to behave better.

To use time-in, bring the child onto your lap or to a "calm-down area" in your home. When my children were younger, we had a calm-down area that consisted of books, a drawing pad, a calm-down glitter jar (see pg. 154), rice for sensory play, and balloons to pop. I would bring my child to this spot and sit with him to do some calming activities. Once he stopped crying or struggling against me, I knew his thinking brain had come back online. You will be able to tell when your child moves from aggression or high emotion to a state of calm and being receptive. Once you perceive receptivity, tell the child briefly what boundary she crossed and how she can better manage her behavior. For instance, if she was tantruming over wanting another cookie, you might say, "You were upset with me, so you screamed at me. I understand you feeling upset, but I won't let you scream at me like that. I don't like to be screamed at, just like you don't like it. The next time you're upset with me, I want you to come to the calm-down area and draw me a picture to show me how you feel."

This is where a paradigm shift must occur for you. I know we've been led to believe that when children misbehave, we should be unloving or cold toward them to show our disapproval. We think we motivate them through scornful looks, harsh tones, and timed isolation, but this doesn't motivate children for the right reasons. In fact, when we remain loving and responsive, even during correction, we build trust and attachment, and it is through that attachment that children will want to be good for us. (Look up the six stages of attachment by Dr. Gordon Neufeld for more about this.)

Some people may worry that time-in is a reward for misbehavior. We only view it as a reward if we believe we must be disconnected to teach. Children only view it as a reward if this is the only time they get positive attention, which is not the case in your home.

If you're dealing with multiple children at the same time, it's a juggling act, for sure. I had two separate areas for my boys, and I just had to go between as best I could. It didn't take long before my children could calm themselves by using the items in their box. With consistency and patience, you'll get there!

Some children prefer to be alone when they are upset. If that is your child's preference, don't force a time-in. As long as the child is actually able to calm himself and get to that rational brain, it doesn't matter where he does it. Just convey that you're available for comfort should he need it, and remember to always wait and teach a calm brain.

More Alternatives to Punishment

1. Take it away

I'm not a fan of removing privileges or items just for the sake of "making them suffer," but there are times when removing an item is the logical thing to do. If my boys are fighting over something, I may ask if they can come to peace or if they need me to step in. If the fight continues, I will calmly and kindly take the item into my possession. They've heard me say, "Your relationship is more important than this toy" so many times they probably say it in their sleep. It's a message I want to sink in. Relationships are top priority. Once they come to an agreement, the item is theirs again.

One time my son broke a boundary we had placed on his electronics use. I did take that particular device away until we had a family meeting discussing the problem and potential solutions. We discussed Internet safety, and he wrote me a report about the necessity of staying within the boundary. Then I gave it back, and we've had no issues since.

2. The peace table

This is a good option for older siblings or when they have friends over. Set aside a child-size table as the "peace table." Teach children to go to this special place to resolve an argument. I'd suggest having a feather known as the "talking feather" on the table. Whoever has the feather has the turn to speak. The other child should listen without interrupting. When the child is finished, she hands over the talking feather and listens to the other child's point of view. You will then talk them through working out a solution until they are able to do this on their own. It might look like this:

"I'm hearing Annie saying she is upset because she was getting ready to use those blocks, and I'm hearing Beth saying that she was already using them and wasn't finished yet. Am I right?" This type of narration helps children to feel heard while also relaying back to them the facts in the dispute. "What is a possible solution? Annie, how about when Beth is finished with the blocks, she lets you know so you can use them? Will that work?"

Children need to stay at the peace table until they've reached a peaceful solution.

3. Pull over

Arguing in the car is a common complaint, and for good reason. It's very distracting for the driver. So, when mine argue in the car, I pull over to the side of the road and sit quietly. After a few seconds, one will say, "Hey Mom, why did we stop?" I reply, "I can't concentrate on the road with you two arguing. I'll drive when you've reached peace." I haven't had to pull over very many times. They caught on pretty quickly. This may not work for some children, who may be perfectly happy to continue their squabble on the side of the road. We all have to figure out what works for our kids.

4. Write it out

Our values are clear in our family mission statement, and our rules are in plain sight. Now that my boys are older, when one breaks a family rule, I ask him to sit with me at the table and write out the rule that was broken. This is to help him commit it to memory. Once he's copied the rule or value, I ask him to repeat it to me, and then if repair needs to be made to a relationship, perhaps with his brother, another family member, or a friend, I will ask him how he intends to make the repair. If he needs my assistance, I provide it. However, this is something I expect both of my sons to carry out with little help.

5. Give grace

No matter how great a parent you are, your child will make mistakes. She is only human. Often, we punish our children just for being human, for having human emotions and reactions that they haven't controlled perfectly, yet we adults don't always control them perfectly either. Sometimes parents yell or slam a door out of frustration, and yes we could've done better and should try to do better, but at the same time, we aren't robots. Sometimes life is really hard and we lose it. What we need during that time isn't for someone to lecture us, but for someone to listen and understand, and many times, this is what children need as well. We shouldn't hold children to a higher standard than we ourselves can attain. Hold them to a high standard, but also be willing to give grace when you can see it's needed. We all make mistakes, and constant correction won't stamp out our children's humanity any more than it will stamp out our own.

Success Stories

I realize that this huge shift in how you discipline can feel too big to swallow at first. You may feel like this will work for some kids, but not yours, or you might worry that a nonpunitive approach will produce undisciplined children. I receive messages often from parents who are thrilled with the progress their children and families have made with positive, nonpunitive discipline. I'd like to share a few stories with you from my readers to uplift you and ease your mind about making this positive change.

Bailey wrote to me to share how nonpunitive discipline was working for her. "I do look back in amazement that we have made it to almost three without having to punish him at all. No time-outs. No shaming or yelling. No spanking or physical punishment whatsoever. He's actually being disciplined and taught with his dignity as a human being respected, and he's not a brat for it! People enjoy being around him, and so do we. More than we ever thought possible, we enjoy him, and we enjoy parenting. Absolutely humbling and remarkable."

Jessica is a member of my Facebook community. She says, "I love how phenomenal the advice is here, and how it's changed my family dynamic. I am a single mother of three kids. Using the tips and techniques from this [Facebook] page, I've been able to lead my children in a much healthier and happier way rather than boss them. I feel empowered and capable now to turn any fight, any lie, any misbehavior or outburst into a loving teaching and connecting moment. That is beyond priceless to me."

Crystal has a fabulous story to share. I always love hearing from readers who have older children whom they have parented positively from a young age. She writes, "We used gentle parenting practices, no punishments or rewards, never hit him, and probably raised my voice less than 10 times. We had lots of discussion and reasonable boundaries. As a preschooler, it was often tricky to keep in mind that it was appropriate for him to be testing and pushing boundaries. I worked to keep the long-term goal in mind. Now, people always tell me how polite, appreciative, and thoughtful he is. He does great in school and makes friends easily. Seriously, I never need to even really discuss his behavior because he just doesn't misbehave, and I think it is the firm foundation of mutual respect we created when he was younger. My advice would be to keep doing what you know works and keep in mind your long-term goals. Now I watch my 11-year-old engage with our toddler, and he is using all the same approaches we used with him. I love that he is gentle with his little brother because he is just repeating the way he was treated."

Rachel wrote to me about her success with replacing time-out with time-in. She says, "During a tantrum, I carry my son to his bed and lie with him until he stops crying. I soothe him and hold him. He calms down really quickly. Once he's calm, I ask if he's ready to talk about it. I always wait until he's ready. He tells me why he was upset. I listen and sympathize. I also help him verbalize his emotions if he's having trouble explaining. Then we talk about how we can both do it better next time. This has worked miracles in our house. He responds so much better to this method. Now we usually don't even get to that point."

Mary shared her success with time-in on my Facebook page: "We began about a year and a half ago and it has worked wonders on the amount of tantrums as well as the length of upset. It took a couple of months to begin to see the effects, but it was a life changer!"

Jennifer's story is one I hope to hear from many more of you. She says, "Positive parenting has changed our entire family dynamic. I feel it has made my husband and me connect so much more in positive ways. We focus on the good in situations, which has allowed our children to see a healthy relationship."

Finally, I have to share with you the comment Erica made to me: "Positive parenting, learning to assume positive intent in my children's actions, not only changed my parenting, it changed my entire heart toward all humans. I've been doing it for 15 years now, and I have kids aged 13, 15, 18, and 20. My older kids testify the difference to anyone who will listen."

I invite you to drop by my Facebook page, Positive Parenting: Toddlers and Beyond, and tell me your success stories. I love to hear from parents whose relationships have been transformed with positive parenting. I look forward to hearing from you!

Discussion Questions

1. When your child misbehaves, who takes the responsibility?
2. Does solution-oriented discipline make sense to you? Talk about what might be the outcome for a child who receives punishment versus one who is given the responsibility to fix his own mistakes.
3. Plan how you will intentionally respond—not react—to the behaviors that you find most challenging. Think of ways the problem can be solved. Ask your child to help solve the problem.
4. Are you willing to switch from time-out to time-in? Give it two months, and if you don't see a dramatic positive difference, you can always go back to time-out.

Putting It into Practice

As promised, here are a few examples of using solution-oriented discipline.

Age: Toddlers and Preschoolers

Scenario 1

Eighteen-month-old Emma wants to explore the electrical outlets. A stern "no" hasn't deterred her, and you don't have any outlet covers yet! Your friend tells you to smack her hand away, but you don't feel right about it. What can you do?

Step one: Look behind the behavior. What is driving it? It's fairly easy to determine at this age. It's just her need to explore her environment. She's curious and doesn't understand this "no" means danger.

Step two: Discipline yourself first. In the case of safety, you're obviously not going to take five deep breaths and say a mantra; you're going to get her away from danger. That might mean a stern "Stop!" to catch her attention until you get to her. Yelling *to* your child to signal danger isn't the same as yelling *at* your child.

Step three: Connect. In this particular scenario, you're just getting your child out of harm's way and teaching her a boundary. She isn't in the midst of an emotional upheaval, so she's probably already feeling connected.

Step four: Find a solution. State the boundary in simple terms. "No outlet. That hurts!" Make your point with exaggerated facial expressions, like big eyes and a pouty face for pain. Ideally, you can get her to divert her attention to something else, but if you have dinner going on, another child to tend to, or some other pressing task, you'll need another solution. If she goes back to the outlet, simply pick her up and take her to a safe area until you complete your other task, such as to her crib or a playpen. If she cries, empathize with her. "You didn't want to go to your crib. I know. But the outlet hurts! I don't want you hurt."

Step five: Restore and reconnect. As soon as you are able, get her out of the playpen or crib, give her some snuggles, and play. Then go pick up some outlet covers and save yourself a world of aggravation!

Scenario 2

Three-year-old Ben has a doozy of a tantrum right in the middle of the aisle because you won't buy him a toy he wants.

Step one: Look behind the behavior. Clearly, the kid is pretty mad. Is there something else going on, too? Is he tired? Hungry? Remember, *look for a positive motive*. He's not really trying to embarrass you to death.

Step two: Discipline yourself. Take some deep breaths. It's probably not even the most exciting thing the other shoppers have seen today.

Step three: Connect and calm. Wouldn't it be nice if stores had a calm-down area? "Ben, you really want the toy. I understand." (Tip: Carry a stress ball, small pad and pencil, or small activity/coloring book in your purse.) Offer empathy.

Offer cuddles. Avoid threats. There are a few things to try in this situation, depending on your child's temperament. Having their feelings acknowledged and being held works to calm some kids. For others, you may be able to calm them with fantasy. "That is an awesome toy! I wish we could buy it. What if we could buy all the toys in this aisle? Wow! What would we play with first?" Yet other children might just need to get out of the aisle, pronto. Take him to the car and wait until he's calm. If you have a full cart, you may just have to let him be while you wheel around a crying kid. I won't judge. Most people wouldn't.

Step four: Find a solution. Basically, just don't call him a crybaby or buy the toy! Be empathetic to his feelings but don't give in to his demands just to stop the tantrum. There's no need to lecture him when you get to the car or punish him when you get home. He didn't get the toy. You held the limit. That's enough. You can talk when he's calm about how he can better handle frustration and anger the next time he doesn't get what he wants.

Step five: Restore and reconnect. The incident is over. Leave it in the past and find a way to laugh and have fun with him.

Scenario 3

Your five- and three-year-old are fighting over a toy. Again!

Step one: Look behind the behavior. They still lack the ability to work out conflicts. It takes time!

Step two: Discipline yourself. You can totally handle this in a very suave, adult manner. Deep breaths. Mantra.

Step three: Calm and connect. If they're fighting, they need to take a break from each other. Have them take some time to cool off away from each other.

Step four: Find a solution. When they've cooled off, try the peace table, or just sit on the couch to discuss solutions. The five-year-old is probably capable of offering some ideas to solve the problem. If not, throw in your ideas. Would they like to take turns by a timer? Is one willing to find something else to play with instead? Does the toy need to be put away? Let them know if a fight erupts over the toy again, it will be put away until they are able to play peacefully, because relationships are more important than toys.

Step five: Restore and reconnect. "I know you love each other very much. It doesn't feel very good to fight with each other. Would you like for us all to do something fun together now?"

Children Over 5

Scenario 4

Your six-year-old screams, "I hate you!" when you hold a limit you've previously set.

> **Step one: Look behind the behavior.** She's angry about your limit and hasn't mastered self-control quite yet. She needs your help to manage that big emotion.

> **Step two: Discipline yourself.** Oh, man, that is a trigger, isn't it? Hurtful words like that can break a mom's or dad's heart. You immediately want to lash out. Or cry. It's best to walk away right now. "That really hurt my feelings. I'm going to take a time-out. You should do the same."

> **Step three: Calm and connect.** When you're feeling ready to talk, you might say, "I understand that you were mad at me. It's not okay to talk to me like that. I love you, and hearing those words hurt."

> **Step four: Find a solution.** Here's where you ask the solution-finding questions: Why did you say that to me? How did you feel after saying it? How do you think it made me feel? How are you going to fix this? What will you do the next time you're mad at me? If you have a connected and trusting relationship, the knowledge that she really hurt you will be consequence enough.

Step five: Restore and reconnect. "Even though you hurt my feelings, I still love you very much, and nothing will ever change that. I forgive you for what you said, and I know you didn't mean it." Do something together that fills both of your love tanks.

This same process is used every time you need to correct your child. Once you've used it so much that it has become a habit, children will automatically start looking for solutions. In my experience, it's easier with older children. When my son was eight, he once stormed off and slammed a door because of a small miscommunication we had. He accidentally hurt my foot, and my reaction to pain made him think I was mad at him. He's highly sensitive, so he became guarded and stormed off. My six-year-old said, "Don't worry, Mom! I've got this." He followed his brother and asked him the questions. He was really good at it, too! My oldest came to me and immediately apologized for slamming the door, and we talked about our reactions.

Sometimes, you may need to remove a toy that's been thrown or fought over, take away an electronic device if your child isn't staying within the limits set around it, or have a child work to replace something. Those are all logical consequences, and I don't want you to feel like you can't use them to teach your child if you feel it's appropriate to do so. Punishment is an unrelated consequence given to a child for the purpose of making him suffer for his wrongdoing. The intent is much different. Consequences that make sense and are given for the purpose of teaching are not going to harm your child. Growing up thinking that there are no consequences for bad choices is more harmful. If part of the solution involves a logical consequence, just be sure to restore and reconnect.

Make a calm-down jar: In a mason jar, add a cup of hot water, two tablespoons of glitter glue, extra glitter as desired, and food coloring. Hot-glue the lid on the jar. Place the jar in your calm-down area. An upset child will often find the swirling glitter very calming, so show her how to gently shake the jar and watch the glitter settle. Tip: To make it swirl longer, add one part corn syrup to three parts water.

10

Top Parenting Challenges— and How to Use Proactive Parenting to Deal with Them

> Children need love, especially when they do not deserve it.   —Harold Hulbert

I RECENTLY SURVEYED a group of more than nine thousand parents, and I asked them what the top behaviors were that made them lose their cool. In this chapter, I'll address those top five challenging behaviors, highlighting proactive parenting, one of the basic principles of positive parenting. By being proactive and preventing these five behaviors up front, you can make sure these challenges don't cause you to lose your cool.

I did say in the beginning that this would not be another book to tell you how you should discipline your children. I offer the following advice only as a guide for moving from conventional parenting practices to positive parenting because I have found that it is helpful for parents in the beginning of their positive parenting journey. Again, though, you know your child better than anyone; you are the expert on your child. My number one advice is always to listen to your heart.

One: Aggression

Topping the list of the five most challenging behaviors is aggressive behavior. Nothing seems to bring out our own aggressive behavior quite like seeing our children be aggressive. Reptilian brain meets reptilian brain. When we meet aggression with aggression—a spanking for hitting a sibling, for instance—then nobody is really in control, and what's worse is that it sends the message that aggression is an acceptable response. This is the time to exercise what you learned back in chapter 2—discipline yourself first. Make sure you're in control of your emotions and that you're responding instead of reacting.

To be proactive about aggression, ensure that the discipline you're using isn't causing anxiety or frustration in your child. Fear often manifests as aggression, so if your discipline methods elicit fear, you could see that fear come out in aggressive behaviors. Use time-in and problem solving in place of punishment. Second, teach your child emotional intelligence. Help her name and understand her emotions and teach her how to manage herself, and she will experience less frustration, which reduces the chance of aggression. Finally, when you allow a child to rest in your love—when she knows there is nothing that could separate her from your love—she will feel safe and connected, and the feelings that cause aggression will diminish.

It's important to realize that children who are aggressive aren't "bad" children. They are often children who are scared, hurt, or feeling disconnected. Very young children do not yet have the self-awareness or language ability to tell us what's wrong, and they may not even know what's wrong themselves. They also don't yet have the mental capabilities necessary to think their actions through. Aggression in older children can be a cover-up for more vulnerable feelings such as fear, guilt, anxiety, or shame.

For very young children, under age five, keep it simple and to the point. Remove the aggressive child from the situation. Take him to time-in (sitting next to you or on your lap) and state your limit. "I won't let you hit. That hurts. I'll keep you and everyone safe until you're feeling calm." The primary focus is to get the child's brain regulated, because remember, when he's resorted to aggressive behavior, his brain is in that fight-or-flight mode, and he's not going to take in your lesson until he's calm and can reach his higher brain functions.

I know this may seem like a reward—some cuddle time with a parent after he's just hit someone. Think of it like this: When you're mad and call on a friend or partner to talk, or when you just take a moment to calm down so you don't act on your feelings, is that chat with a friend or taking that moment alone a reward for your anger? No, it's emotional management, and it's an important skill to learn. During this time, you can be empathizing with your child's emotions and helping him verbalize what he's feeling and what made him angry. This teaches him emotional intelligence.

Once the child is no longer angry, restate kindly and firmly the "no hitting" rule and discuss alternatives (walking away, etc.) and what will happen if he hits again (leaving the playdate, for example). Recall that this child is under five. It's going to take time for him to master emotional control. The last thing you want to do is to pin the label of "naughty" or "aggressive" on him. Remember, children see themselves through the eyes of their parents, and they will try to live up (or down) to those expectations, for better or worse.

It's also important to get into the habit of looking for the root cause of the behavior. A consequence is just a temporary Band-Aid, but getting to the root cause and addressing it brings true healing. If you notice your child is aggressive because of jealousy, then you can address the jealousy and the aggression will subside.

For children ages five to eight, their executive brain functions are getting better and it's time to start problem solving. This teaches them accountability, emotional intelligence, and positive conflict resolution skills. It may look like this:

Brenna is six, and she just smacked her younger sister. After checking on little sister, you take Brenna to time-in. "Our rule is no hitting. Tell me what happened." Brenna explains that little sister was annoying her. You can say, "What are the three things we went over that you can do when you're feeling upset? You can take deep breaths. You can walk away. You can ask me for help. But you may not hit your sister. Tell me the three things you can do again." Listen while she repeats them back to you. "Okay, good. So the next time you get frustrated with your sister, what are you going to do?" She'll probably say one of the three calm-down techniques. "Good. Now, I think your sister is feeling upset that you hit her. Look at her face. What does her expression tell you? How are you going to fix this?" If she doesn't offer any ideas, give her some. "You could write her a note, or make her a drawing, or apologize and give her a hug. Which do you think will make her feel better?" This teaches her that she's the one responsible for repairing the damage she's done, and it gives her the tools to do it.

If a child over the age of about eight is showing aggressive behavior, find out what's going on inside him. What is that aggression covering up? If you feel your child is showing aggressive behaviors that are extreme or sudden and out of character, seek professional advice.

Two: Whining

Some parents view whining as the different voice a child uses when she wants something. Others mean incessant asking for what the child wants after he's been told no. Both types of whining can certainly grate on a parent's nerves, so let's address each one separately.

Whining in which a child uses a different voice is actually a more mature form of crying. Scientists have found that our brains are hardwired to respond to the sounds of a baby's cries. In fact, the emotion centers in our brains light up in about a hundred milliseconds after we hear the cry![18] Whining is just a step up from crying and still provokes a visceral reaction that urges us to take action to make it stop. Only now we don't see a helpless baby. We are generally perceiving a child trying to manipulate us, because isn't that what we've been told for ages? You've noticed by now that I talk a lot about perception, and that's because how we perceive our children is key to how we interact with them. If we can switch from feeling manipulated to seeing a small human trying to get needs met (which is what she is), then we can come to this situation in a calmer state and do a better job of teaching.

Many experts recommend simply ignoring the child when she whines, but I don't believe ignoring the people we are close to does anything positive for our relationship. So, let's go over some concrete steps you can take when your child is whining.

1. Listen. Often, children just want to feel heard and understood. Show empathy for the child's upset. This can be hard to do when our brain is screaming, "Make it stop!" However, the more we practice empathy, the easier it becomes.

2. Look for the reason behind the behavior. Children may whine for all sorts of reasons, and their whining may actually be a cry for connection or help. It may simply be a release of pent-up emotions, or maybe he's tired or overwhelmed or hungry. Meet the need behind the behavior, if you can discern what it is, and the behavior will cease.

3. Provide lots of preemptive cuddles and laughter. Did you know that laughing releases the same built-up negative feelings as crying? Spending some time every day giggling and connecting will reduce whining.

Let's say your child is a bit older, and you suspect she is whining simply because she thinks you'll give in to her requests if she nags you. Here are some tips to nip that type of whining in the bud and empower your child with better communication skills.

1. Teach your child the difference between a strong voice and a whiny voice. She may not even be aware that she is using a whiny voice. You can do this through play with puppets or

toys to show her the difference. When she begins to use the whiny voice, tell her to please use her strong voice.

2. Give her some control. Some children whine because they feel powerless. Make sure your child knows she is a valuable part of the family and give her choices throughout the day so that she feels she has some control over her daily life.

3. Teach negotiating skills. This will alleviate the feeling of powerlessness that triggers whining while also teaching your child an important skill. Teach her to state her needs and wants in a respectful manner and how to work to find solutions that will satisfy everyone's needs. If she wants to go to the park but you have dinner to cook, then you may negotiate that she will help you with dinner and you will take her to the park afterward. If your child knows you will listen and take her needs and wants seriously, she will feel more important and connected, and the need to whine about things will dissipate.

4. Don't give in. Once you have established that you will take your child's requests into consideration, then you've also established that no means no. I tell my children, "I will always say yes when I can, but when I say no, I mean no." If they ask again, I simply say, "You've already asked me, and I've already answered." When they realize that will be the consistent response, the whining stops.

Be proactive to prevent whining by:

- Offering choices
- Validating emotions

- Teaching the difference between a strong voice and a whiny voice
- Invoking your child's imagination. If she's whining over going to the park but it's a rainy day, say something like, "I bet you wish we could make the rain stop with a silly dance and use a giant hair dryer to dry up the world. Would a hair dryer work?"

Three: Not Listening

When parents say, "My child doesn't listen," what they usually mean is, "My child doesn't do what I say when I say it." Am I right? In my experience, children are almost always listening (try whispering something random when you think they're not); however, they may not respond, and that's frustrating. We want our children to cooperate without having to ask them five times to do something. So, what can we do to make that happen?

Ironically, the way parents typically try to gain cooperation from kids actually causes them to tune us out.

Ironically, the way parents typically try to gain cooperation from kids actually causes them to tune us out. Nagging, lecturing, counting, and demanding do nothing to foster cooperation. Punishment or the threat of punishment may compel a child to act, but that isn't real cooperation.

Always keep the connection strong. If you have a child who rarely listens (i.e., does what you ask), then you may need to work on your connection with that child. Generally, people want to help others when we feel good about them and about ourselves. How much quality time have you been giving him? Next, look at what and how much you're expecting of him. If you're asking him to stop in the middle of an amazing Lego construction to go take a bath, then it's understandable that he may not hop to it. His mind is very involved in his play, and it's hard to switch gears quickly for most children. Be reasonable and respectful, just as you'd want others to be to you. "I see you're building an awesome tower. I want you to take a bath in ten minutes." Give him another notice at five minutes before bath time. This gives him time to transition and is just generally a respectful thing to do. Remember how you feel when your child demands another juice when you're engrossed in something else? Show him courtesy, and he'll learn to show it back to you.

Sometimes things can't wait. I get that. If something really needs to be done and done now, here are a few tips to increase cooperation.

1. Use a firm and respectful tone at a conversational distance. Barking commands from across the room, or across the house, is much less effective than walking over, getting your child's attention by initiating eye contact, and then speaking.

2. Use "I want" statements rather than "will you" statements. "Will you pick up your toys now?" leaves an option for "No." It's a question, not a request. "I want you to pick up your toys now" says that this is not negotiable.

3. Ask once, then take action. Few things are more annoying than asking a child to do something several times and not getting a response. So, don't ask him several times. State your request in a kind and respectful tone once, make it short and clear, and ensure you have eye contact or at least listening ears by asking if he heard what you requested. If he doesn't do what

you told him to do, then take action. This means if you told him to put his clothes away, go over to him, make eye contact, and say, "It's time to put your clothes away." Guide him toward the laundry pile and ensure he gets it done before you leave the room. Yes, I know this takes a lot of effort, and I realize you want him to do it the first time without you having to monitor him, but this is more effective in the long run. If you ask once and then act, he will very soon learn that you expect him to listen the first time. If it continues to be a problem, go back to the first thing—the relationship. If you keep asking to the point that you lose your cool and yell, then he begins to understand he doesn't really have to do anything until you start screaming. So, by putting a little more effort in at the beginning, you will save yourself a lot of frustrating moments in the future.

Be proactive to prevent cooperation problems by:

- Focusing on keeping the connection strong
- Being mindful of transitions and giving the child appropriate time to comply
- Not repeating yourself over and over. Teach your child to listen by taking action after the first request once reasonable time to comply has passed.

Four: Tantrums

Our *perception* of tantrums, not the tantrums themselves, is really what pushes our buttons. We perceive them as defiance, manipulation, or bratty behavior. The truth is that most tantrums, particularly in young children, are simply a child's way of expressing emotions that have become too difficult to handle. Children don't like having tantrums any more than we like seeing them. If we can change our perception of tantrums from defiance to a call for help, we can approach this behavior in a way that is both helpful to the child and strengthening to the parent-child relationship.

A little research into child development reveals that children lack self-control because of an underdeveloped prefrontal cortex, the part of the brain that regulates emotion and social behavior. What happens is that your child feels a strong emotion, such as frustration or anger or sadness, and, not knowing what to do with this strong emotion, her brain goes into panic mode known as "fight, flight, or freeze." We've all had this happen. Have you ever been so upset that you slammed a door? If it's difficult for adults to control their emotions all the time, imagine how much harder it must be for children, who are still learning and developing.

Conventional advice is to ignore the child during a tantrum, but this really sends the message that we aren't there for them when they're upset, or worse, that we only accept them and want them around when they show feelings we like. No one wants to be ignored when they feel distressed. We are social beings wired to connect, so connect with the tantruming child, if it helps soothe her. Hold her in your arms while she offloads all those negative emotions. If you're worried this will "reward" the tantrum, think about a time you were extremely upset and a partner or friend empathized with your upset or held you while you cried. Did it make you want to feel upset again? Of course not. No one likes to feel upset or out of control. **Empathizing with children during a tantrum is not rewarding behavior;**

it's meeting a need—the need for connection and understanding. If affection and empathy seem to only fuel the flame, then back away and just let her get it out. You can let her know you'll be close by when she's ready for a cuddle.

Empathizing with children during a tantrum is not rewarding behavior; it's meeting a need— the need for connection and understanding.

While it is critical to support your child through a tantrum, it's important not to change your position if that is what triggered the outpouring of emotion. Giving in to her desires will teach the child that your limits are negotiable. Hold the limit while showing empathy for your child's feelings.

Concerning older children, whose prefrontal cortices are better developed, it is still important to empathize while holding your limit because this sends the message, "I hear you, and you matter." The simple act of not giving in to the demands prompting the tantrum will soon teach the child that his behavior won't work to get what he wants. If the tantrum is not a real outpouring of emotion but rather a play for power, ignore the behavior, *not the child.* This means that you don't intentionally give the cold shoulder, and you're not having any sort of reaction to the tantrum whatsoever. You're simply neutral toward the whole thing. You're not letting his emotional reaction cause you to have an emotional reaction. If a school-aged child tantrums in a way that is aggressive—hitting, kicking, or throwing things—this is a clue that the child needs emotions coaching or some kind of help, not punishment. During the tantrum, ensure everyone's safety. That may mean putting distance between the aggressive child and other family members. You might say, "I see you are very angry. I won't let you hit.

Take some time to calm down in your cooldown zone." Once the storm has passed, address the aggressive behaviors. Explain that his feelings are acceptable, but his actions are not. Teach him how to manage his frustration and anger with techniques such as deep breathing, counting, going for a walk, or clapping to release energy. Punishing children for tantrums won't help them learn how to manage them. Until we give children better tools to deal with tough emotions, we can't expect them to do better.

Be proactive to prevent tantrums by:

- Assuring your child has had enough rest and enough physical activity
- Being aware of tantrum triggers (overtiredness, hunger) and preventing them
- Using time-in or a calm-down area. Over time, your child will learn to calm herself before she erupts.
- Teaching emotional intelligence. When she has the words and ability to express her emotions, tantrums will lessen.

Five: Back Talk

The way parents handle back talk in early childhood sets the stage for whether or not this will be a recurring problem when the child is older. All children will occasionally challenge their parents, but by having a respectful and connected relationship, you greatly reduce your chances of this turning into a chronic behavior problem.

It's important to note that in early childhood, children are only beginning to learn to separate from their parents and assert themselves. What many parents consider back talk can be better understood as the child's need for autonomy. Positive parents respect this need and teach appropriate, respectful ways to communicate.

The most important thing we can do first and foremost is to set a good example. This means we model respect in our interactions with our children. If we are prone to yelling, they will be as well. If we choose to ignore their requests without explanation, they will learn to ignore ours. We must set the example for how to communicate respectfully.

When your requests are nonnegotiable, word them as statements, not questions. Young children think in literal terms, so if you ask, "Will you put away your toys?" the child will interpret it to mean there is a choice. Instead, try saying, "Put your toys away now, please." If your request is met with "No" or "I don't feel like it," remember she's asserting herself and learning to voice her opinion. This doesn't mean you take no for an answer and pick up her toys for her, but it means you understand it isn't about defying you so that this doesn't trigger your anger.

You can make a game of beat the timer for young children or use "When . . . then" statements such as *"When* your toys are picked up, *then* you can go outside to play." For times when your child keeps arguing with you about a limit you have set, do not bicker with him. Acknowledge what your child is wanting, validate his feelings, explain your reasoning once, and then use a short and respectful statement to disengage from the argument, such as "I've already answered that" or "I won't be arguing about this." If you're experiencing hurtful or rude comments from your child, such as "I hate you" or "You're stupid," understand what she's really saying is, "I'm upset and don't know how to handle this." All feelings are acceptable, but not all behaviors are, so let your child know that you hear her and understand she is upset but that she needs to find another way to express it. You might say, "It's not okay to speak to me like that. I understand you're feeling upset, but speak in a way that doesn't attack me. If you can't do that right now, take a break and come back when you're ready to." Don't blow it up or show a strong reaction. Over time, with proper teaching and understanding, your child will learn how to identify those feelings and express them appropriately.

Keep in mind that children learn conflict resolution skills by being in conflict with someone! If it's always your way or the highway and the child doesn't get a say, how is she going to learn? Learning to effectively communicate her side of things is a good skill to have, so let her practice it sometimes. "Why is this important to you?" "What other ideas do you have?" "This is the reason I'm saying no."

Here are the three keys in handling back talk.

1. Listen to what is behind the words and discern what is really motivating the child so that you can take the personalization out of it. This deactivates your trigger of feeling disrespected.

2. Empathize, which shows the child that you listen and care about what he feels and wants (a behavior you'll want him to pick up) while holding your limit. This will dissipate the power struggle.

3. Listen and keep an open mind. If you're willing to hear your child out and possibly even change your mind after a good debate about it, you're not a weak parent. You're being flexible,

reasonable, and respectful. If it's really nonnegotiable, state why and then politely end the conversation.

Be proactive to prevent back talk by:

- Teaching your child positive communication skills, as we reviewed in chapter 4. Teach her to state her view respectfully and how to accept no for an answer.
- Have you been too controlling or too permissive? Both elicit back talk.
- Apologize if you've been disrespectful to your child in the past, and set a new standard of respect.

YOU WILL FACE many challenging behaviors throughout your journey as a parent, and if I've learned anything as a mother, it is that *time* is often the solution. As children grow and mature, phases come and go. I have already been through many phases with my children, phases that I thought would never end, phases that I thought would break us, phases that made me question everything I was doing as a parent. I know that there are many more phases to come in my parenting journey. I take comfort in one truth, and my heart breaks at that same truth: It all ends.

You've heard it before. This is not a revelation. You know that they will grow fast, but often in the bleary-eyed and exhausted days of early parenthood, we can wave off this fact as not being helpful in the moment. Believe me, I know that what you want is help, time alone, a full night of sleep, and a day without crying—not someone telling you to just enjoy every second because it goes so quickly. I understand how that can feel patronizing in the moment. I'm saying this to you from my heart, and if you really let this truth sink in, it will help you in the hard times.

The tough phases do end, and with the end comes relief but also a bit of heartache when you realize they need you a little less than before. Time cannot be slowed. Hard phases cannot be rushed and good phases cannot be frozen; we must take it as it comes and do the best we can with the bad and savor as much as we can of the good, because there is no stopping it either way. That little boy or girl will grow up, and your role will be redefined many times over. That is both the beauty and the sadness of parenthood.

My sincere hope is that this book has helped you grow individually and helped bring you together as a family. I hope it has strengthened your family bond and given you a focus for the future. Mostly, though, I hope that you close this book with the same determination that I am closing it with now as I write these final words—the determination to be the best parent you can be and to build relationships that nurture souls, because in the end, relationships are the most important things we acquire in this life, and none are more important than the lasting bonds we build with our families.

Putting It into Practice

Proactive parenting is one of the core principles of positive parenting. By being proactive about preventing the top five behaviors we've discussed, you can make sure they don't cause you to lose your cool.

- Start teaching emotions management very early, even before aggressive behavior starts. Talk about what your child can do when she's angry, and give her easy-to-remember tools to manage anger, such as stomping, clapping, or jumping up and down.
- Set a clear rule against aggression and violence, and enforce it consistently.
- Teach children to use their strong voice. Show them the difference between a strong voice and a whiny voice.
- Teach them how to state their wants respectfully.
- Give children choices throughout the day so they feel that they have some control. This helps to eliminate whining and tantrums.
- Prevent public tantrums by making sure your child is not too tired or hungry. Take breaks throughout a long day of being out and about with stops at a park or a place to run free. Be clear about what you expect and what your child can expect when you go out.
- Teach positive communication and conflict-resolution skills.

A Word
of Encouragement

Dear parents,

Building your connected family will be a journey. May I advise you not to expect this whole raising-a-person thing to go off without a hitch? There will be roadblocks and detours. Troubles will come and go. Being connected doesn't mean being perfect; it means loving each other through the imperfections.

Remember that while positive parenting does ask you to be intentional and to grow yourself, it doesn't expect perfection. You won't be the perfect mom or the perfect dad. Your kids won't be the perfect kids. And that's okay! Fortunately, all the unconditional love and grace that's afforded to your child through positive parenting is also afforded to you. When you slip and fall, help each other up and keep on going.

Keep a baby picture of your child close by always. When times get hard, look at that picture. When your child is running you ragged, when you feel like you can't take one more minute, pull out the picture and look at it. Look at the eyes and remember the feeling you had when you looked into them on that first day, when those eyes first gazed up at you and took your breath away. Those are the same beautiful eyes you look into today.

Friends and family may not agree with your parenting choices. They may think you should be tougher. They may think you're spoiling your child. Rest assured, no one has ever turned out wrong because he or she was cared for too much. Forget what they say and stay focused on your mission: building your connected family. There is no such thing as too much love and attention. Not for your partner or for your children. Shower them with it every single day because none of us knows what tomorrow will bring.

I don't have all the answers to all the questions I get asked, but I do have a solution for pretty much every problem in life: love. Love your people. Your partner, your kids—those are your people. Love them well and don't hold back. A life spent loving well is a life lived well. I promise that you will never regret giving your love.

One final piece of advice. When you lay your head on your pillow at night, ask yourself this one simple question: Did my people go to sleep tonight feeling loved and valued? If the answer is no, get up and do something about it. Or at least resolve to make tomorrow night a different story. If the answer is yes—Yes, my people went to sleep tonight feeling loved and valued—then rest easy, sweet parent. You're doing all right.

With love and gratitude,
Rebecca Eanes

To My Beloved Child

I promise to love you courageously for the rest of forever. I will guide you with wisdom and grace. Come with me, my little one, and we will learn and grow together.

I will honor your childhood and your dignity.

I will always see the light in you, and I will reflect that light back to help you find your way. You are safe here, my love. Rest.

You are free to be you, wholly and completely, and know that you are wholly and completely loved for who you are.

Your smile lights up my world.

Your laugh makes my heart sing.

Your wonder helps me to see.

Your joy lifts my spirits.

You are teaching me so much about life. I am grateful for you.

I will always be your encourager. If you need reminding of your goodness, strength, courage, or resilience, call on me. I am here.

I hope you know what a miracle you are. You are unique, one-of-a-kind, my blessing.

May you live with peace, compassion, joy, and love as a result of the peace, compassion, joy, and love you've experienced here.

Notes

1 Segal, Jeanne, and Jaelline Jaffe. "Attachment and Adult Relationships." *Helpguide.org*. Helpguide.org, n.d. Web. 28 Dec. 2014. <http://www .helpguide.org/articles/relationships/attachment-and-adult-relationships. htm>.
2 Segal and Jaffe.
3 Luby, Joan L., Deanna M. Barch, Andy Belden, Michael S. Gaffrey, Rebecca Tillman, Casey Babb, Tomoyuki Nishino, Hideo Suzuki, and Kelly N. Botteron. "Maternal Support in Early Childhood Predicts Larger Hippocampal Volumes at School Age." *Proceedings of the National Academy of Sciences 109.8* (2012): 2854–9. Web. <www.pnas.org/cgi/ doi/10.1073/pnas.1118003109>.
4 Siegel, Daniel, and Tina Bryson. *No-Drama Discipline*. New York: Random House, 2014. Print.
5 Graham, Linda. "The Neuroscience of Attachment." *Linda Graham, MFT, Resources for Recovering Resilience*. N.p., n.d. Web. 13 July 2014. <http://lindagraham-mft.net/resources/published-articles/the -neuroscience-of-attachment/>.
6 Cook, Gareth. "Why We Are Wired to Connect." *Scientific American*. Nature America, 22 Oct. 2013. Web. 28 Dec. 2014. <http://www .scientificamerican.com/article/why-we-are-wired-to-connect/>.
7 Castelloe, Molly S. "How Spanking Harms the Brain." *Psychology Today*. Sussex Publishers, 12 Feb. 2012. Web. 28 Oct. 2014. <http://www .psychologytoday.com/blog/the-me-in-we/201202/how-spanking-harms -the-brain>.

8 Fentress, Debra. "Neural Pathway Restructuring." *Neural Pathway Restructuring.* N.p., n.d. Web. 14 July 2014. <http://www.neuralpath wayrestructuring.com/home.html>.

9 Gottman, John. "What Makes Marriage Work." *Genius.* Genius Media Group, n. d. Web. 11 Feb. 2015. <http://genius.com/John-gottman-what -makes-marriage-work-annotated>.

10 Lisitsa, Ellie. "The Four Horsemen: Criticism." *Gottman Relationship Blog.* Gottman Institute, 29 April 2013. Web. 9 Feb. 2015. <http://www .gottmanblog.com/four-horsemen/2014/10/29/the-four-horsemen -criticism?rq=four%20horsemen>.

11 Cannon, H. Brevy. "U.Va. Study Identifies Four Family Cultures in America." *UVA Today.* University of Virginia, 15 Nov. 2012. Web. 20 Dec. 2014. <https://news.virginia.edu/content/uva-study-identifies-four -family-cultures-america>.

12 Hurley, Katie. "Is Low Self-esteem Contagious?" *Everyday Family.* Everyday Family, 8 Dec. 2014. Web. 20 Dec. 2014. <http://www.every dayfamily.com/slideshow/low-self-esteem-contagious/>.

13 Goleman, Daniel. "Family Rituals May Promote Better Emotional Adjustment." *New York Times.* 11 March 1992. Web. 20 Sept. 2015. <http://www.nytimes.com/1992/03/11/news/family-rituals-may- promote-better-emotional-adjustment.html>.

14 Markham, Laura. *Peaceful Parent, Happy Siblings.* New York: TarcherPerigee, 2015, p. 167. Print.

15 Brown, Brené. *The Gifts of Imperfection: Let Go of Who You Think You're Supposed to Be and Embrace Who You Are.* Center City, MN: Hazelden, 2010. Print.

16 Brown, Brené (BreneBrown). "Shame corrodes the very part of us that believes we are capable of change." 20 March 2013, 5:21 p.m. Tweet.

17 McLeod, Saul. "Carl Rogers." *Simply Psychology.* Simplypsychology.org, 2007. Web. <http://www.simplypsychology.org/carl-rogers.html>.

18 Jha, Alok. "Why Crying Babies Are So Hard to Ignore." *Guardian.* 17 Oct. 2012. Web. 11 Jan. 2015. <http://www.theguardian.com/science /2012/oct/17/crying-babies-hard-ignore>.

Acknowledgments

I WISH TO thank the following people for their contributions to this book:

To my agent, Sandra Bishop, thank you for believing in me. What a blessing it is to have you at my side.

To my editor, Marian Lizzi, and the team at Perigee, it has been a great pleasure working with you. You've made this entire process enjoyable, and I'm grateful that you believe in my message.

To my friends Amy Bryant and Rachel Macy Stafford, who were my listening ears and provided me a shoulder to lean on. Thank you for encouraging me.

To Kelli B. Haywood for reading through the manuscript and offering your valuable advice. You always came through when I was in a pinch, and your encouragement gave me strength to keep going. Thank you.

To all of my sweet friends who have supported my journey. I cherish each and every one of you. When I wanted to give up, you cheered me on. You are true blessings. I am forever grateful.

To the Positive Parenting: Toddlers and Beyond Facebook community, thank you for your support. Every post you have shared has helped spread the message of positive parenting. You are changing the world.

I have been inspired and enlightened over the years by the work of Dr. Laura Markham, L. R. Knost, Lu Hanessian, Lori Petro, Janet Lansbury, Dr. Dan Siegel, Dr. Tina Payne Bryson, Gordon Neufeld, Becky Bailey, Patty Wipfler, and many other advocates for positive, conscious parenting. Thank you for showing me a better way.

To my amazing community of conscious parenting advocates, each of you has inspired me and helped me grow. Thank you to Alison Smith, Amanda Rue, Amy McCready, Amy Phoenix, Andrea Nair, Andy Smithson, Ariadne Brill, Bridgett Miller, Casey O'Roarty, Eric Greene, Genevieve Simperingham, Jacqueline Green, Josh Kitzmiller, Katie Hurley, Lelia Wes Schott, Marilyn Price-Mitchell, Nicole Schwarz, Susan Stiffelman, Alissa Marquess, Chelsea Lee Smith, Dayna Abraham, Shawn Fink, Leslie Potter, Samuel Martin, and many others! It's a blessing to know every one of you.

To the amazing family I married into, I am forever grateful to call you my family. Thank you to Roma for all the advice that was spot on in helping me become the mother I need to be, and especially for raising the amazing man who is now the father of my children. I hope to do as well at this parenting thing as you did.

To my parents, Sharlyne and Teddy, who have supported and encouraged my writing since I was a little girl. Thank you for believing in me. I wouldn't be where I am today without your love and support.

To Gavin, my Doodle Bear. You are the reason I chose to follow a different parenting path. You have taught me so much more than I could possibly teach you in this life. Thank you for helping me grow. You inspire me each and every day. Know that you are a bright light in this world, and it needs you. You are a blessing.

To Aiden, my Little Bear. Your unconditional love has inspired me to be a better person. I hope to love and live as fully and joyfully as you do. You spread happiness everywhere you go. You make this world a better place. Thank you for making me laugh a million laughs.

To my dearest husband. Twenty years and counting, my love. You've shone the light so I could find my way out of the darkness. You've celebrated with me and cheered me on every step of the way. You are my very best friend. Thank you for being the kind of daddy our boys can truly aspire to be like. I love you always.

Thank you, God, for your love, mercy, and grace. You are the ultimate example of unconditional love.

About the Author

Photo by Charlee Lifestyle Photography

REBECCA EANES IS the founder of Positive-parents.org and creator of the Facebook community Positive Parenting: Toddlers and Beyond. She is the author of *The Newbie's Guide to Positive Parenting* and *Positive Parenting: An Essential Guide* and coauthor of *Positive Parenting in Action: The How-To Guide for Putting Positive Parenting Principles into Action in Early Childhood*. She is a contributing editor for *Creative Child Magazine* and *Baby Maternity Magazine*.

As a mother who made the paradigm shift from traditional parenting to positive parenting, Rebecca shares inspiration and her hard-earned wisdom daily through her rapidly-growing Facebook community. Seeing how the power of connection transformed her own family inspired Rebecca to share this message with other parents in hopes that they, too, may find more closeness and peace.

She is married to her high school sweetheart and loves capturing miracle moments every day with her two sons.

Also by Rebecca Eanes

THE

POSITIVE
PARENTING

WORKBOOK

An Interactive Guide for
Strengthening Emotional Connection

Rebecca Eanes

Author of *POSITIVE PARENTING* and creator of Positive-Parents.org